ATTRACTING IN ABUNDANCE

Opening the Divine Gates to Inviting in
Blessings and Prosperity Through
Body, Mind, and Soul Spirit

KEVIN HUNTER

WARRIOR
OF LIGHT
PRESS

Warrior of Light Press
www.kevin-hunter.com

Body, Mind & Spirit/Spiritualism
Body, Mind & Spirit/New Thought
Self-Help/Motivational & Inspirational

WARRIOR OF LIGHT
POCKET BOOK SERIES

♥

Contents

PART 2: OPENING THE FLOODGATES
OF ABUNDANCE

AUTHOR NOTE

£ike many of my books, *Attracting in Abundance* is infused with practical messages and guidance that my Spirit team has taught and shared with me revolving around many different topics. The main goal is to fine-tune your body, mind, and soul. Like all souls, you are a Divine communicator capable of receiving messages and guidance from Heaven.

My Spirit team makes up God and the Holy Spirit, as well as a team of guides, angels, and sometimes Archangels and Saints. I am merely the liaison or messenger in delivering and interpreting the intentions of what they wish to communicate. My team comprises some hard truth telling Wise Ones from the other side, including Saint Nathaniel, who can be brutal in his direct forcefulness. He cuts right to the heart of humanity without apology. I have learned quite a bit from him while adopting his ideology, which is Heaven's philosophy as a whole. I wouldn't preach Divine Guidance that God doesn't whisper into my Clairaudient ear first.

If I use the word "He" when pertaining to God, this does not mean that I am advocating that he is a male. Simply replace the word, "He" with one you are comfortable using to identify God for you to be. If the word, "God" makes you uncomfortable, then substitute it with one you're more familiar with. This goes for any gender I use as examples. When I say, "spirit team", I am referring to a team of 'Guides and Angels'.

One of the purposes of my work is to empower, enlighten, as well as entertain. It's to help you improve yourself, your soul, your life and humanity by default. It does not matter if you are a beginner or well versed in the subject matter. There may be something that reminds you of something you already know or something that you were unaware of. We all have much to share with one another, as we are all one in the end.

~ Kevin Hunter

THE
ATTRACTING IN ABUNDANCE CURRICULUM

*A*ttracting in Abundance is broken up into three parts to help move you towards inviting abundance into your life on all levels.

Part One contains some no-nonsense lectures surrounding the philosophies, concepts, and debates on the laws of attracting in abundance.

Part Two is the largest of the sections geared towards fine tuning your soul into preparing for abundance.

Part Three is the final lesson in the abundance curriculum to assist in opening the gates of abundance with various helpful tidbits, guidance, and messages, as well as the blocks that can prevent abundance from flowing in.

PART 1

Philosophies, Concepts, and Debates on the Laws of Attracting in Abundance

KEVIN HUNTER

CHAPTER ONE

The Vibrational Discord Between You and Abundance

When one hears the word abundance, they may automatically equate it to being blessed with a plentiful overflowing amount of money, finances, and riches that equates to a big lottery win. Having enough money to survive comfortably enough on this physical plane is part of obtaining abundance, but it's not the destination purpose to thrive for. You could work hard to make enough money to the point you are set for life, but that won't necessarily equate to happiness. The journey should be enjoyed as much as reaching the destination. If it's not, then what will happen once you reach that destination? You'll be constantly starving for more obtainment.

Human beings have been trained and taught to accumulate material and physical gratification over anything else. Thriving to create and produce what you love is one positive element to abundance, but this is about the obsession to achieve more finances. Chasing a dollar to have more money you do nothing positive with is not a goal to thrive for. For some it becomes hyper mania to obtain additional finances even though they are already financially comfortable enough for life. If there are any positives to chasing finances, it is to improve the quality of life for yourself, which subsequently enables you to be free to help others. This might be done through things like humanitarian work, charity giving, or you have a staff to employ and need to take care of. By that turn, you're ensuring the survival of more than one person that relies on that paycheck to pay their bills. At the same time, chasing anything usually pushes it further away from you. It's the nature of the way energy attraction tends to operate.

The intention God has for your soul on Earth is to thrive spiritually. You may not be a spiritual person or have any spiritual or religious beliefs, but you are having a spiritual experience regardless if you believe in anything beyond your physical body. When your life run is up and your body dies, your soul carries on with the knowledge and lessons gained through that one life experience. Your soul will not take any material or physical content that you've collected during this lifetime. The intention Spirit has for you is to crave ongoing knowledge during this temporary Earthly living situation set up. It is not to settle for mediocrity or the superficial that your human peers feed others daily for consumption. What's being fed to the masses may be what results in being a number one top trending mark on the social media charts, but the second you die all of that is obsolete and worthless.

The darkness of ego loves drama and gossip, both of which give one a temporary high that pulls it out of boredom. A human being that shuns boredom is usually due to partaking in productivity. They are too busy being creative to pay attention to what the masses are complaining about on social media.

Your soul's higher self is the closest element to God. Deep down your soul desires spiritual fulfillment that cannot be filled up through temporary superficial vices, material, physical, or instant gratification. In my twenties, I was the master at experiencing desires when I wanted it, but like the spiritually based U2 rock song I would keep saying afterwards, "I Still Haven't Found What I'm Looking For."

This is because those passing pleasures were still leaving me empty. The ego, or the Devil as some call it, says that you don't need to continue working to improve. His intention is to hold you back and keep you down. He cannot stand it when you seek to achieve knowledge, raise your consciousness, and rise above and beyond human shallowness. When your soul grows smarter and more equipped, then he loses a potential soldier to the Light.

Certain countries continue to frown upon women from learning. The United States used to be like that through history on up until the 20th century when the breaking point was scheduled to push that and much more out into the open. Enormous technical progress was made in a large way during that century including the change in many attitudes leaning more towards accelerated progressiveness compared to centuries past. This has its blessings and challenges. The 21st century is destined to see chaos, drama, and corruption due to the rapid way that information is spread through a technical device. On the one hand connecting with others is made easier, but on the other hand it invites in perpetual "noise" as my guides call it.

I've forever been fascinated with taking things apart to see how they function and operate. This carries over to my interest in the human condition from as early on as childhood. This included me asking the deeper questions. Why do groups of people behave a certain way while together, but behave differently as an individual? The complex dynamics of how one operates is captivating. I like to get into the brain chemistry mechanics of understanding how it functions from one person to the next. This assisted me in becoming a master at the complex art of studying the psychology of human behavior.

When the higher self's soul is not running the show in its Earthly life, then it is the ego in the human physical body that is dominating. From a basic standpoint, human beings function in a primal manner, much like animals in a jungle. Human beings move in herds in a single file, which to one extent is basic common courtesy etiquette. Most people tend to telepathically know to stay on one side of a sidewalk as another person coming towards them is on the opposite end of the sidewalk. When driving a car, you're trained to stay in your lane, even though I'm sure you may argue that some don't even do that. Friends have visited certain foreign countries like in the Middle East where there doesn't seem to be any laws of driving. They've informed me it's complete chaos with horns consistently blaring angrily. People driving in wrong lanes while others are gunning it on foot in the middle of the road amidst the sea of cars aimed in different directions. Imagine what that does to your psyche over time.

When we're not observing common courtesy etiquette of a single file line, then chaos is born through the aggravation of senselessly bumping other souls. The second you bump into another person, both of your energies have latched onto one another. If it was a toxic person you walked passed in this manner, then some of your Light energy has touched them. The challenge is some of their toxic energy has infiltrated your aura, which you will carry with it throughout the day unless you release it immediately.

Human beings in general have their basic day-to-day routine of waking up, getting ready for the day, hopping in the car dressed up and moving with the pack to get to their jobs. People will mark their territories and surroundings the way an animal might. They will get possessive of a mate the way some animals in the animal kingdom do. They will fight to dominate and obtain power the way certain animals do. There are a wide variety of complex emotions that are affected by the surroundings of human beings. This can cause the soul confusion as it attempts to navigate through life in the most comfortable way possible. For the more sensitive and in tune souls, they'll experience this aggravation on a higher level. On the one hand a psychic sensitive person can be a gift, but the curse is moving through the Earthly jungle with others who aren't as in tune, and instead overstep their boundaries with you.

Like animals in the jungle, human beings are in a human jungle they created on God's creation. They will operate in ways that are similar to that of an animal in a jungle. From that perspective, it can appear to be somewhat caveman like, perhaps even barbaric and animalistic in some circles or areas on the globe, and almost limited in another sense. It's interesting that many long to have a world where everyone is accepted, but when you examine how people behave, you find they adapt to the culture and surroundings of their physical environment.

When someone desires people to behave on the planet, what they sometimes mean is they want them to have the same values and behavior traits as they do. We all do it to one degree or another, and most of the time we're not even conscious of it. Sometimes what others insist on is helpful and on the mark. This can be noticed when you take a step back to examine what they're asking others to do that can be positively beneficial for all involved in the end.

There are a small percentage of people within individual cultures and tribes that will break away from that. Transcending out of the group mentality they were trained and developed in early on. Sometimes they may flee that group only to place itself into another group that they will go along with. Hopping from one reality and into another version of their current reality, but never truly finding their authentic soul self. Even if they find that tribe, they may still withhold certain personal views for fear of being ostracized, judged, and criticized by certain members in this new group. Somewhere in this physical human casing there is a soul consciousness that has the ability to rise above certain animalistic characteristics and see the broader picture.

The soul has the capacity to absorb a wealth of knowledge. It has the power to bring in what it desires into its current reality. This starts with a thought, a dream, and a foresight that begins to grow and expand into an intensified crystal clear vision. What many are longing or fighting for in this human jungle is a profusion of love and abundance.

Seeking abundance is not a new concept and nor is it one that the spiritual new age communities invented, even though it's been made popular in modern times by the spiritual communities. The longing for abundance goes back to biblical days. There are numerous positive quotes and passages pertaining to abundance in the controversial book that is both loved and hated called the Bible. It includes passages that urge you to follow Christ in order to reap rewards and gifts. He wants you to have an abundant life, which is more than the quest for financial earnings or money.

Some religions detest the abundance and law of attraction theories discussed in spiritual circles, but in essence they are also lured into this abundance seeking. They want the physical material rewards and gifts as well, which is why they follow Christ. Non-believers also desire rewards and gifts, which is why they are also drawn into teachings of abundance. This is all because it is basic human nature to want some measure of material to survive on the planet.

Most every conscious being is aware you need to make money to be able to obtain food, clothing, and housing. If it's a struggle to attain those basic human survival necessities, then life can be stressful. Therefore, it's understandable that you long to be able to have enough finances to comfortably survive. One of the first steps for all human beings is the awareness that you need to obtain money to physically survive. All in Heaven understand this plight as well too. You're not a demon because you long and need to make money to endure. It's only when that longing and need turn into greed that it falls into a deadly sin. Not the kind of sin where you'll be sent to Hell. This sin falls into the realms of the true darkness you're pulled under through a misguided quest that results in getting your soul nowhere in the end.

The traits of happiness and love are traits that

every soul on the planet personally longs for. It's become a struggle for many to reach that state of happiness. They wind up chasing after butterflies and mirages that appear to be enticing as the answer to revealing these riches. The density of the Earth's atmosphere places enormous pressure on the soul that causes communication blockages with the Divine. It messes and tampers with your emotions in trying to find that centered space of peace where you have everything you could ever want. You spend your entire life pursuing those pretty dreams hoping and praying for some blessing or miracle. The answer is in your hand, in your mind, and in your feelings. It is in your soul burning like a raging fire screaming to make that Divine connection where you are transcended into an authentic feeling of joy, love, and peace.

True abundance in the eyes of God, Higher Beings, Heaven, myself, and my Spirit team's perspective in modern times is more than longing or dreaming of having boundless money filtering through your life. This is the case even though it's understood that money is needed to make certain things happen in life. It's needed to physically survive on the planet. You have to pay your rent or mortgage, you have to eat, you need clothes to wear. Those are considered necessities and essentials for basic human survival. This doesn't include physical body upkeep from Doctor's appointments to Dental appointments. There are people who don't have access to either of that.

True abundance is living an existence where you are functioning in the highest soul vibration possible. You are filled with God and Spirit's love. It is overflowing to the point that you experience upbeat high vibrational emotions like joy, peace, and love. It is impractical in today's world to be in that state non-stop every second, even though you can imagine how awesome life would be if that were humanly possible.

You are human right now living an Earthly life with physical longings and desires to feel comfortable. You have emotions and thoughts that move up and down from the positive to the negative and back around again. Even the happiest joyous person on the planet will feel sad, angry, depressed, or stressed from time to time. This is all dependent on what's taking place in your life on any given day.

It can also be dependent on whether you battle with mental health issues. There are statistical claims pointing to 450-500 million people battling some form of mental health disorder. That should come as no surprise as it's an insane world with never-ending noise and issues taking place every single second. Most of that at the hands of other people and with a great deal of that in front of you on places likes social media and news sites. If you were the only person on the planet, sure maybe it might get a bit lonely, but you can also likely admit that it would be somewhat on the peaceful side. There would be no arguing, fighting, whining, stirring up drama, gossip, or trouble. You'd more than likely be residing in some state of serenity.

If everyone followed the mantra of functioning without stress, obscenity-ridden judgments, and instead chose to live in a joyful peaceful compassionate state, then this would be a utopian paradise. This is unlikely to happen anytime soon. Especially considering that the planet is centuries and more into humanity's progression and life on Earth, and yet the globe is still unable to revert to love as the core manner of communicating with others. Discord has been ripe with relentless fury since the first human beings walked the Earth. It has never lightened up.

Humanity has a tough time in thinking and feeling in love. This isn't about being 100% positive 24/7, as that is an impossible feat even if your general disposition is a happy content positive one. It does mean going back to the mantra that if you don't have anything nice to say, then don't say anything. It does mean that when you're experiencing negative or challenging anything, then take the time to move through that. Examine what it is that has taken place in your life that has thrown your world off kilter.

As you run your life like a strict executive, look to see if the upset is warranted or misplaced. If you were on your way to work and got into a car accident, then yes your upset is warranted. If a top trending story is a controversial one about a public figure you don't know personally, then your upset is misplaced. Your feelings and thoughts in your day to day world have a profound effect on whether or not the flow of abundance is moving towards or away from you, so be mindful and aware of your overall state of being.

CHAPTER TWO

Creating an Abundant Life

Having an abundant life might be something that makes you happy and gives you daily pleasure. It can be filled with good positive-minded friends who accept you unconditionally no matter how many skeletons you reveal. There is nothing you can say that would make them write you off. Your mutual loyalty is sacrament to the both of you. I would be the first to help a friend bury the body. Not everyone can truly say that and mean it. Especially today where people are quickly writing one another off if a flaw is revealed or if their choices are not exactly like yours. If they vote politically a certain way or have a different spiritual view, you could be kicked out of someone's life with the snap of a finger. They quickly write others off when what they believe to be any imperfection is revealed. That's not mafia like loyalty at all, but a loyalty riddled with conditions. Having that kind of rigid stance with your own clan will block the positive flow of abundance from coming in.

Some of my best friends may partake or have participated in behavior that I don't condone, but I don't write them off. It's pretty known that my anti-cheating or anti-adultery stance is pretty strict. Yet, I have friends that had committed adultery in their life at one point. It doesn't mean I kick them out. Accepting people's differences takes an immense amount of work. No one is exactly like anybody else and people are going to do things that are disagreeable to you. How you choose to accept that and not take it personally can have an effect on how successfully you navigate through those Earthly life hiccups and challenges. One of the repeated phrases I've heard from friends and those around me are, "I feel I can always tell you anything and you don't have any judgment at all. I don't know anyone else that's like that."

An abundant life today can be about having more good times, fun, and laughter. Laughter raises your vibration up into God's vortex. You can feel your vibration has risen when this happens. Your vibration is your overall well-being state. If you're feeling low, then your vibration is low. If you're on cloud nine and filled with happiness, then your vibration is high.

You've likely had one of those laughing fits at some point in your life. You were also able to detect how that made you feel and the feeling was good. You could feel it through your entire being. Suddenly you were walking on clouds happy on life. Some have commented that they could sense that infectious wonder just by hearing someone else's laughing fit in the vicinity. Maybe it happened while you were at a restaurant, in a movie theater, or at work. You smile and look at whomever you're with and share a telepathic acknowledgment that this laughing fit you're hearing is irresistible.

The laughter and joy is an example of what raises your soul vibration. When your vibration is raised, then it reaches that threshold where abundance flows in. This is why it's important to bring these little things up as reminders as to what can help in accelerating the flow of good things in your life. It doesn't mean you're going to be drama and challenge free.

God can mean diverse things to different people from a higher power, the Light, Spirit, the Universe, and so on. My own life was less dramatic and less challenging when I devoted my life to God full time. It included incorporating all of these little tips to the point that I noticed a grander shift happening. It was too obvious not to notice the positive changes and results that were surfacing. I, and my Spirit team, have been sharing a great deal of them with others throughout my work for the benefit of those interested or ready for it.

An abundant life can be about partaking in work that excites you and brings out your passions. This is also similar to finding your life purpose and diving wholeheartedly into that in the right spirit. It enables you to have enough time outside of that work you do to spend with friends, family, and loved ones, or whatever activities you find pleasurable. This is pending it's not harming you or another person.

Some find anything associated with the word *pleasure* to be evil. You're not intended to have a miserable life. Pleasures and playtime fun are essential in making sure you're not overloaded with constant stress or that you don't experience burnout. This isn't about the kinds of pleasures that are considered toxic, dangerous, or unhealthy. It might be to go on a hike with a friend, or a fun road trip to a destination far enough away from home to feel as if you're getting away, but close enough to get to. It can be that you have enough time to take regular breaks and see places you've always wanted to visit and explore. It can be watching a movie that entertains, inspires, and helps you escape a hard circumstance for a spell. It can be spending intimate time with a lover. You have that beautiful blissful loving soul union relationship with someone, which makes your life feel abundant.

Having an abundant life can be having enough income to be able to live problem and worry free without fear of never being able to pay your bills or purchase practical necessities to survive. You've reached that place in your life where you are no longer struggling. You can choose the area you've always wanted to live in. You can buy that home of your dreams. You can and may even obtain all of that and much more, but you may still feel unfulfilled. Without a strong spiritual connection with something greater than yourself, you can be left feeling empty even after achieving and obtaining those material physical pleasures and desires. There are countless cases of people who fought hard to achieve materialistic abundance, but were still left feeling just as empty as they were before obtaining those things.

In Madonna's lone wolf spiritually based album titled, *Ray of Light*, in the song, *The Substitute For Love*, she writes and sings the words, *"I traded fame for love without a second thought. It all became a silly a game, some things cannot be bought. I got exactly what I asked for. I wanted it so badly. Running, rushing back for more, I suffered fools so gladly. And now I find I've changed my mind."*

She sought out and chased fame and fortune, and achieved that and more in a big way. She later admitted she was still feeling empty and unsatisfied. There are similar cases reported where someone was chasing material physical pleasures and desires. They obtained all of that, but were still feeling low and unimpressed.

Many purported to say they found that happiness in a strong spiritual connection, whether that is a connection with Jesus, Buddha, God, the Universe, or Spirit. It doesn't matter what you call it even though in some spiritual circles they may do their best to make you feel guilty, bad, and might even bully you for not following who they personally follow. This is not about them or what they want for you. This has been especially the case in extreme organized religious organizations. That behavior is what has chased followers and people away from those systematic human made created religions. Because of their bad behavior and judgment on others, they pushed people away from Christ. Now people hear the name *Jesus Christ*, and they cringe. They assume he is the one casting the judgment, when his love is all love. The harsh judgment casting was coming from his misinformed followers that wallow in the darkness of ego. Out of thousands of pages in a book, they only follow a few passages. They only use those passages to use as ammunition to attack and condemn others. This is not being spiritual or of Christ.

Statistics have popped up showing a never-ending decrease in religious followers because of this. They've chased some people to the further extreme of atheism. Although now more people today are finding a stronger connection with God in the spiritual communities, which angers extreme religious followers and atheists. Extremist religious people have great disdain for anyone that is not strictly and religiously following the Bible word for word, even though many of them cherry pick and choose what they want to follow themselves. They will use the excuse that it is okay as long as they ask God for forgiveness for their wicked ways.

There are a great number of people that walk in both worlds of the spiritual and religious. They are some of the most content and centered people I've met because of that balance. They might praise

Jesus while being supportive of people no matter their race, political affiliation, gender, sexual orientation, and on and on.

Some of the extreme sides of spirituality or religious disagree with someone being able to walk in both worlds, but that just means they're unable to or choose not to. They don't have a say in what you decide is best for you. This is your life and when you walk with God, you are able to be more of an efficient manager and owner of that life. No one else can claim that power, even if they use the Bible as an excuse to justify their insistence on you changing to bend to their ways. They don't have the market cornered on what God wants for you.

Regardless of your spiritual beliefs, you are trained early on by society and your peers, to achieve a high status of popularity and fortune. Some abundance teachers and motivational preachers ask you to sign up for their seminars so that you can too can work where you want and still have enough time to travel the world freely. People chase those practical monetary dreams. While some may achieve it, they continue to fight to achieve more physical desires long after the achievement. Many remain unhappy and stressed out. They haven't figured out that this is not working for them. They're unhappy because they're merely going along with what they were trained early on to seek. At the same time, you understand the need or desire to at least be making enough of an income that you can live comfortably without fear of not being able to pay your bills.

Perhaps you have a large calling and purpose

guiding you to partake in work that is not only your passion, but it is a purpose that has a snowball positive side effect of helping others. The problem is you don't have enough time to devote to it, because you work a full time day job that does not fulfill you in any way. You want to quit that job so you can participate in the work that means something to you. You can't quit that day job because you need an income to be able to pay your rent, buy food, clothing, and practical necessities. You know you have to quit in order to focus solely on your passions and life purpose, but that is not a realistic move, so you wind up feeling stuck. You could look for another job to get out of the life force draining one, but you also know you may end up moving from one poor circumstance to another.

Money doesn't solve the problems of happiness, but it does help to have enough to physically survive. And in that scenario described, having enough income where you don't need to work a time and energy sucking full time day job with toxic people is not an outlandish desire for a physical being.

The good news is there is a glimmer of light at the end of that dark tunnel. Devoting just a small amount of time each day or week towards your passions that you desire to be lucrative can give you something to look forward to. There are many success stories where someone lived that way and reaped in positive benefits. Add to that daily prayer and asking for heavenly guidance gives this a greater shot and making this dream come true.

There are also stories about those who were in a situation like that for years. They worked hard on their passion and purpose on the side while at a day job they despised. Once enough of a steady income was coming in with that passion purpose side work, they were able to comfortably quit their day job without fear or worry, and partake in the work that truly is their passion and love.

Regardless of what your finances are like, you are the manager and creator of your life. When you team up with God and your Spirit team, then there is no telling what you can accomplish. You can decide how you will act or react to something someone says or does. You can choose the job you want to look for to an extent. Sometimes you may end up accepting a job you don't really want because you have bills to pay. You are still choosing to make that temporary sacrifice by accepting that blessing of a job. No one is putting a gun to your head. You are doing the best you can in managing your life with the resources you have at this juncture in your life.

Achieving a utopian abundance life state is what the soul desires because it reminds it of home where everything was blissful and peaceful. It's like you moved from a mansion overlooking paradise in Heaven to a rundown apartment on Earth for a brief time in your souls existence. You did so for the sake of evolving your soul. Your soul doesn't evolve much unless it has to endure rough experiences for the purpose of lessons learned. When you learn a lesson on Earth, then that means you learned from the mistake. When you learn from a mistake, you grow and work on not doing it again. Some get stuck in that cycle of repeating the same mistakes until they notice the pattern and snap out of it. This way they can move onward and forward.

Even the most miserable person on the planet longs for happiness deep down inside the core of their soul. Happiness being subjective since one person's version of the happiness they desire could differ from another ones.

There are people who have evil fantasies of world domination and that would make them happy. This of course is not the kind of abundance God and my Spirit team speaks of or the kind you're even thinking about. This is also what they mean when they say happiness is individual based.

One person could desire a home, the love soul mate marriage partner, the kids, and a good job. Those requests would fulfill their physical desires. For another, they may not care about any of that, but want the freedom as a single person to roam about the world and travel to see the different parts of the globe and dive into higher culture learning.

Longing for that authentic abundant life feeling starts from within. You fill yourself up with overflowing happy thoughts of abundance. Your emotional state feels like you're riding sky high above the clouds. It's to live a utopian existence that would be possible if people behaved themselves and fought to function through life in a high vibrational state. Most the chaos and turmoil created is at the hands of other people or

KEVIN HUNTER

conjured up within you. Your goal should be to reach this utopian paradise state, but then transcend even higher than that. When you are in the epicenter of that vibration, there is no telling what kind of bountiful abundance would come flowing in.

26

CHAPTER THREE

Attracting in Abundance

*T*his is a physical world that requires money to survive. If you don't have any money or physical related survival requirements such as food, clothing, shelter, then persevering through life can be challenging and sometimes even catastrophic. There are millions of homeless adults and children in the United States alone. This doesn't include the homeless around the world. There are also people who are employed, but are also homeless because the money they're making isn't enough for adequate housing. There are other roadblocks preventing them from obtaining a space to rent. There are people that live in impoverished regions around the world that will never breakaway from that kind of life no matter how positive their thoughts are.

A woman from India informed me that when she was visiting her homeland of India while on a train ride through the country, it travelled through areas where there were masses of people just sitting on a hill. It was jam packed with so many people that there was barely a space to walk. That's where they live so they just hang out there all day and night.

This is where some skeptics take issue with all of the magical whimsical abundance teachings pushing this abundance concept on others, and rightly and realistically so. This is because a great many people around the planet will never achieve anything remotely close to this kind of material manifestation. From that perspective, it almost comes off arrogant or entitled to believe that while you're doing okay in life, you're not in a situation where climbing out of that would be impossible, such as living in an impoverished area.

Many in western civilizations want to climb higher than where they are at now. They're driven by money to the point that they want more of it. They want to live in the lap of luxury in mansions and large SUV's while being free to purchase material items on a whim or travel around the globe lounging by a different pool on another island with a cocktail in their hand.

There are millions of people that swear by the law of attraction. There are also millions of people that find it to be ridiculous new age hocus-pocus. There are those that find it to be evil and of the Devil, especially if you don't follow Jesus Christ. Being too extreme with anything is intolerant and inflexible, which doesn't attract anything good in because there is no balance or middle ground.

No human being has the market cornered on what is right or wrong morally. They might have the morals they were taught by their caregivers or by those around them, or there are the morals they read in a book that insist you should follow these strict rules, otherwise face an eternity burning in Hell. There are the default morals that all should follow, which is treating everyone with kindness and compassion, yet only a small percentage truly follow and display that mantra. There are those that have had the audacity to condemn the kindness and compassionate by saying that's not enough to keep you out of Hell if you don't follow the Bible word for word.

The flipside of the extreme is being too flexible that you invite anyone and everything in, which doesn't attract anything good in either. One factor to include on your quest for giving and receiving a positive flow of abundance is balance and moderation. Be a skeptic until you dive on in and conduct your own research, which means also being a skeptic with some measure of an open mind. This open mind allows you the opportunity to be flexible and open enough to accept far-fetched, yet tried and true methods that help you achieve personal and soul success. Find the middle ground by being adaptable, but careful and cautious as you move forward. That's an example of how to remain neutral, objective, balanced, and in the middle.

Sometimes those that despise the law of attraction feel that way because it doesn't or did not work for them. It can be understood why some despise it and why some swear by it. There are valid reasons on both sides of the spectrum.

Those that despise the law of attracting abundance might be scientific and analytical types, and perhaps at times a bit jaded. I certainly fall into that category, but I dove on into the practice as early as childhood. I won't and cannot discuss something that did not personally work for me. There are also those that loathe the attraction law due to being let down by life's disappointments. They may have tried it and it just didn't work for them. You can sense the anger when anyone brings up the law of attraction. They have enormous distaste for the entire spiritual community because of that. This is where their argument can get lost in a sea of nonsense. They don't know about everyone's trajectory or the struggles they've had to endure. They don't know how the one struggling overcame hard times and ended up attracting in more positive experiences into their life. If something doesn't work for you that doesn't mean it won't work for someone else that follows the basic principles of attracting in abundance.

Having faith includes believing that even if things don't go your way or pan out the way you expect them to, you still have hope and remain faithful that what is intended to happen by God will come on the wings of Divine Timing.

There are sometimes reasons beyond your understanding or control as to why an abundance request isn't fulfilled. No one was born into an Earthly life so that they could hand over a list of demands to God that you're going to need if you're going to be here. Heavenly beings have no interest in entertaining someone who has the mentality of a diva movie star with a list of demands that are automatically granted by the film production studio that has cast that actor in their film. God and Spirit don't care about your ego or what the lower self part of you wants. If it takes a soul a lifetime to figure out the meaning of life, then that's how long it will take.

The first two decades of my life on Earth were met with child abuse and struggle. As I moved from my late teens to early twenties, I fell into an addiction to drugs, alcohol, pills, and cigarettes. When I turned 23, I got that lucky break in the film business where the abundance door was starting to open. I took that as a big sign that something major was being handed to me and that I can't blow it. That was more powerful than any toxic addiction, so I simultaneously began the process of dissolving those hardcore addictions.

The good stuff in my life didn't just land in my lap. I had been trying super hard to get a job in the business behind the scenes from the age of 16. I knew that I wanted to get into the business. That visualization was always there. I psychically saw me in it. I had extreme confident optimism about it. Eventually, after hard work and persistence, having faith, and believing, I caught the attention of the right company that just happened to be owned by a well known movie star. This is to illustrate a small example of how the law of attraction works.

I can understand why some swear by the law of attracting abundance. They desire and long to be happy. Some may become intoxicated by the allure of bright magical happy things that some in abundance circles speak of. I get it. Me too! The part of me that loves that dreamy magic is my Sun in Pisces, but the part of me that is analytical, critical, and realistic about it is my Rising in Virgo. I'm always in a tug of war between the practical and the spiritual. I believe you can conquer your dreams (Pisces), if you work hard and put in unstoppable effort and work ethic into it (Virgo). I've conquered my dreams and attracted finances too many times to count over the course of my life thanks to following the abundance laws.

The one thing to note was that finance accumulation was never my goal or thought process. I never thought, "I'm going to make this amount of money." Money never crossed my mind, but I was mildly aware that ultimately you need some of it for physical survival. I just wanted to partake in work that I deemed enjoyable at that particular time. I went after the work I did because I wanted to do that work. I was even willing to do it for free. The money that came with it was just a positive side effect.

This same thing happened for some that were once poor and rose up to the rich and famous life status. Many of the super talented serious about the craft crowd have admitted they were never seeking popularity or money. They just wanted to be able to partake in their creative art expression. Some of them were pushed into the limelight and paid well, but that wasn't their goal.

The message in that is to go after your passions and your dreams. Seek to partake in work that has meaning to you. This is where you would do it for free if you had all the time and money in the world to easily partake in that. When you find that, then the money will more often than not come in. When you dive into work that pleases and makes you happy, then that moves you into a high vibrational state. When your vibration is high, then you become a positive abundance attractor, so you keep attracting in more even though that was never the goal.

It's called the law of attraction, but in theory it's more of a spiritual law. The law word is metaphorical that if you follow some of the principles, then you're more likely to reap success. I've been following, studying, and testing the principles since I was a child. It wasn't something I sought after or fell into. I just had a grave understanding of some of what it would take to achieve abundance through spirit and God.

Recently, I found a ton of old journal scrapbooks of mine in boxes that showed some of my writings as a pre-teen and teenager. Having forgot them I was stunned as to what I was reading. They were along the lines of philosophical empowering content, which cemented the truth that the information has always been with me. In those days, there was no Internet or social media. The spiritual movement wasn't popular yet. Any traces of it in those days was non-existent to minimal and on the minority side. Regardless, the basic Divine Guidance information had come through me from as far back as a teenager in a shockingly profound way through all of the scribbles in these notebooks.

I may use the abundance or law of attraction words due to it being the fad label of the times that everyone understands, but for me it's much deeper than that. Abundance spiritually is being filled up by the Holy Spirit and the Light first and foremost above all other things. That's what drives the soul to positively achieve.

Money will not make someone permanently happy, but if you don't have any money, then enduring Earthly life can be difficult. If you don't have enough money to be able to freely breathe, and do what you've always dreamed of, then life can be more challenging. This isn't about desiring a sedentary life. It's also not saying that going after money is healthy. It's just saying that you need some amount of an income to eat, have a place to live, and clothe yourself. Those are basic survival necessities on Earth that can't be twisted or avoided no matter how much someone might try to.

At the same time, whatever your state of mind is before money, then it will be the same after obtaining money. If you're miserable before you've attained money, you'll be miserable afterwards. If you've always been in great spirits, then that will continue long after the money comes in. The more money you have, then the more issues that can arise depending on your personality, mindset, spending, and lifestyle habits. If you end up buying a home, then it will come with more responsibility and issues over living in a rented apartment.

Money is just a colored piece of paper that humankind placed a higher value on. That's because we know that this particular piece of paper has the power to purchase material goods you need or desire. It has the power and value to purchase clothes, food, and housing, etc. It has the power to make sure all your bills are paid leaving you free of worry over that.

There are people who live paycheck to paycheck and just barely make ends meet. This is after living a highly budgeted life that includes only purchasing basic survival necessities. They dream of what it would be like if their income could just increase if even a little bit. They dream of what it would be like to suddenly strike it rich having enough money that they could quit their full time job that is making them miserable and slowly killing off their life force.

Various polls and statistics of those in the work force have revealed that about 70-75% of them on average hate their job. Many work full time jobs that don't bring them pleasure on any level. They work at jobs that don't fulfill them. They work at jobs with duties they find dull. They work at jobs with a toxic boss, toxic colleagues, or in a toxic environment. They work at jobs just for the money and the paycheck to survive. It helps them pay the rent, buy food, and necessities. That's a ton of time to spend each day and each week working at a place that makes you miserable in the end. If you woke up tomorrow to find out you are a millionaire, would you quit your job? If the answer is yes, then that means the job is not your passion or life purpose, but one you do with the goal of physical survival. Naturally, it is understandable to see why many become hypnotized over achieving an abundant life. They want to get unstuck from the misery they're currently in. I understand this as I've been there too. With the guidance of my Spirit team, it prompted us to write the book on it called, *Living for the Weekend.* Certain books are mentioned for those interested in more info on that particular content.

BE STRONG IN FAITH

Attracting in abundance includes having a strong connection with God, or whoever you deem to mean God to you, whether it is Spirit, the Light, the Universe, Jesus, and on and on.

I've always had a strong faith in place since I was a child. This is not the same faith in the Devil's work, which condemns you, makes you feel guilty, bad, or fearful. Faith in God is an overflowing warrior like inner strength that you know without a doubt you are filled with the Holy Spirit. You start there and work your way out.

Money is an illusion with no long running purpose for the soul. The benefit that Spirit and

Heaven understand about money is to the extent that it can help you be worry free from physical survival, such as being able to pay your rent or mortgage. It won't remove any other traces of worry such as work or personal relationship issues. This is to name a couple of instances where it can still bring you grief or stress.

Spirit is not of the sort to condone accumulating riches for the sake of it. This guidance is targeted to the ones that already have money and have a comfortable life, yet are continuously driven to accumulate more. Unless the accumulation of more money is with the intent of doing good with it, such as you and/or others end up positively benefitting from it for their own survival. This might be that financially driven CEO type who is running a business and needs the accumulation of finances to keep others employed.

If someone is creating jobs for other people, then this counts as accumulating money for the sake of helping others, even if their mindset isn't in that space. By default they are helping others get employed, which keeps those people out of the cycle of struggle or off the floor below, which is ultimately homeless and in the streets.

There is a limit to how much money one should desire. This limit is so that you have enough to live comfortably to the point that you don't worry about not having a place to live, clothes to wear, or food to eat. It's having enough that you're able to do some good with it. It's having enough that you no longer have to worry about working a day job that doesn't fulfill you on any positive level. It's having enough so that you have more time to devote towards your life purposes and passions.

The accumulation of money isn't to have enough that you turn into a slacker who lounges on a beach with a cocktail indefinitely. Not that there is anything truly wrong with that scenario once in awhile. Could you realistically do that for five years straight every single day? I'm sure even that would grow stale and uninteresting by the end of the first week.

Where will that soul be at the end of its life for having accumulated riches young only to live a pampered spoiled life helping no one in need. Abundance preachers can entice the soul strictly for the allure of doing nothing while having a fat bank account. This shouldn't be confused with the soul who worked hard throughout their Earthly life and are enjoying early retirement.

This doesn't mean that someone of any age shouldn't enjoy their life. Why should someone have to wait until senior retirement to have a few good years left? This is about balance and detecting what is morally or justifiably wrong. Spirit understands that those living on Earth are living on a planet that requires money to adequately physically survive.

Spirit's view of abundance is much more than money. Most everyone desires money because they can buy things they've always longed for. What does it mean for you to have more money? What would you do if you suddenly came into enough money that you wouldn't have to work a day job that sucks out your life force anymore?

Attracting in abundance is more than attracting financial prosperity. Some of the incoming abundance may include that, but this should not be ones sole desire, except to the extent where it's enough that you are able to work on your life purpose without the stresses of having a mundane day job you do for the money. It is not of the Devil to desire enough money to be able pay your bills and live comfortably enough that you can focus on your life purpose and in growing your soul.

This is not about some of the other kind of abundance that preaches about get rich quick schemes. The kind where you live a life of luxury spending your days laying back in a chair in the earlier scenario mentioned of the lush paradise island with a drink in your hand. Doing that indefinitely would no doubt eventually grow boring, but it would also cause you to fall into one of the deadly sins of sloth mode, which is a vibration dropper and abundance killer.

The kind of abundance Spirit talks about is being rewarded for your tireless hard work. This is not about obtaining cash in order to spend frivolously. This abundance is also more than financial. It is about feeling abundant inside regardless of what's in your bank account or the physical materialistic items you own.

One of the theme elements I loved in Disney's *Cinderella* feature was that Cinderella may have been poor and ruled over by a mean stepmother and stepsisters, but she remained a good person, friend, faithful, and hopeful. She was more of a pleasure to know and be around than anyone else in her life. She did her best to do what was needed to survive. A magical spirit godmother appeared granting her a reward and gift that included one night of fun at a dance ball being held at the town's palace. The godmother organized a way to get Cinderella transportation to this ball since she had no way of getting there. Noticing that Cinderella was dressed in torn rags, the Godmother looked her up and down realizing that something was still missing.

Cinderella said, "That's okay. This is more than I could've ever hoped for."

The Godmother repeatedly humbled by this spirit soul said, "Bless you, child."

Cinderella didn't expect anything, because it was the life she was living and it was all she knew. She grew not to expect much if anything at all, but to have faith and optimism. Cinderella ended up inheriting much more than she thought, simply through the genuine act of this humility. I know this is from a fairy tale, but the theme can still be applied practically and has been a thousand times over. Someone wrote that fairy tale and managed to incorporate the basic attraction principles without realizing it. It's an interesting clever way that Spirit can work through others, which is through entertainment pieces.

CHAPTER FOUR

*Debunking the Law of Attraction:
Skeptics and Believers*

You may or may not wonder why devote a section to debunking the law of attracting in abundance. It might seem a bit counter intuitive to the overall positive intent of this piece. It's always been important that we discuss both sides of anything when and where it's possible. This is part of the role of the Wise One. It's also why they make exceptional judges, because they can remain in the middle while deeply going into both sides with incredible depth. This is something that not many want to do, but are capable of by doing the work.   The overall nature of humanity is to pick a side and stay there, while antagonizing someone on the other side of your belief system. That's been going on since the dawn of humankind. It will continue until humankind comes together as a collective to move towards the middle where balance and moderation exist.

All souls have the capacity to move towards the middle of the road if they choose to. The darkness of ego will do whatever it can to keep you from understanding others that walk a different path than the one you're currently on. The ego only wants to talk about their side. If your opinion is a different one than someone else's, the ego doesn't want to hear that. In order to be an exceptional leader, judge, or mediator, one needs to exercise an emotionally distant, yet rational compassionate understanding of someone with a dissimilar point of view. If someone shouts their opinion at you, then no one of sane clear mind would attempt to reason with the unreasonable. The sane mind would walk away from that energy.

Being balanced is looking at all aspects of a situation while reserving the ego's personal thoughts and feelings about it. You look at why someone might feel one way about something, and why someone else feels entirely different about that one thing. Change in humanity can happen when the majority raises their consciousness to that sweet spot in the middle. This is where the soul takes the angels view, which is that of non-judgment of all sides listening to what opposing parties are bringing to the table.

Wanting, desiring, and visualizing millions of dollars is not enough to attract in millions of dollars, and neither is putting a fake check on your fridge with the amount you want to attract in. It can certainly help than hurt for the purpose of helping to motivate you, but that's one mildly helpful start towards attracting in a flow of abundance.

Someone can choose not to partake in visualization exercises and work hard at their job and end up raking in the money. All they did was remain focused, persistent, and hardworking at their job. There are stories of people who don't believe in or buy the law of attraction business, and yet they are attracting it all in. While someone else may have bought every abundance and law of attraction book or CD they could get their hands on, but are still in the same spot they were before they bought those materials.

Some have expressed negativity towards spiritual teachers that have the Doctor title before their name, because the teacher received the certificate from a less than prestigious school or education system. Someone went to further their studies and were doctored. It shouldn't matter where they were doctored or received the certificate from. The point should be that they were interested in studying and improving themselves and this was the way they choose to do it in. Envy towards others successes and endeavors creates a block with the Divine and simultaneously abundance.

I'm typically drawn to people that have street smart experience, because those are the ones that got their hands dirty, got out there, and just did the work, rather than thinking about maybe one day doing the work. If you think about writing that book, but will do it later in life at the right time, then you may never write that book.

There is an infamous motivational quote that is centuries old that says, don't put off tomorrow what you can do today.

The Secret was a popular book and movie that kicked off an entirely new law of attraction movement craze, even though the law of attracting in abundance has been around for centuries. Some of the other myths that debunkers to the law of attraction assume is that those who are fans of *the Secret* or *Law of Attraction* are sitting around waiting for the abundance to land in their lap just wishing. Perhaps there are people who are doing just that, but I certainly hope they are doing more than thinking and visualizing. Otherwise they could be doing that indefinitely with no foreseeable change in anything.

Others have taken offense to the *vibration* word, but someone's vibration is the energy essence you're vibrating at. Are you giving off joy and serenity, or stress and anger? That's all the vibration word means. It's easier to say the word *vibration* than to get into a long lengthy thing, as I tend to do anyway. To have contempt at what works positively for someone else will ensure a block is formed. That energy is unable to attract in anything good, so you may as well work on leaving people alone if it works for them.

There are the *skeptical spiritualists*, which

sounds contradicting, but isn't if you understand the terminology. They are spiritually driven and have an understanding of some of the concepts that are realistic, but they will be intelligently skeptical and questioning of anything that doesn't make sense to them at that point in their life. It doesn't necessarily mean they write it all off, but they will dive in with further study to see if it's nonsense or a concept that works for them. They are open minded enough to study it, but won't take it verbatim just because someone tells them it works. This is more or less how I've been since I was a child. I question everyone and everything to have a graver understanding of something, then I dive into getting the hands on experience until I have a grasp on it.

As a lifelong Clairaudient, I have been hearing God and my Spirit team in my left ear for as long as I can remember. It was through that act that I instantly knew they were real. The reason this is what convinced me early on as a child was because the information they were feeding me was coming true. Regardless, I continued to test them because it is the scientific analytical way I approach anything and everything. We can blame that on my Virgo Rising.

In Buddhism, they ask you to question everything and not accept anything at face value. Do the work, test it out, and see if it works and if you've had success with it. This is better than automatically debunking something that sounds too out there for you to understand when you dive deep beneath the big cliché spiritual words used.

The lower mentality is to debunk everything you hear or read without further investigation and study. This is also all over the media and social media with the masses automatically rushing to negative judgment without deeply knowing anything about what they're talking about.

There are some who read all the law of attraction and abundance books they can get their hands onto. They listen to lectures and attend seminars on the genre. Despite all that, some of them have said they were left with a ton of information being fed to them that they attempted to do something with and apply to their daily life, but it never conjures up anything. Cut to years later, and they're nowhere closer to attracting in abundance than they were when they were initially hypnotized by the abundance notion. They feel as if they spent years throwing away money and energy. They come to the conclusion that the law of attracting abundance movement just does not work.

You can either be lucky at conquering your dreams or you're not. Putting in some effort to take what you've learned and applied what you've picked up on that makes sense towards your quest for fulfillment is far greater than throwing in the towel and debunking the entire theology. Especially since so many have done the steps required with the law of attraction and achieved incredible success.

The law of attraction may not have worked for you to date, but it has worked for someone. That particular successful person might not have equated their success to the idea that it was part of the law of attraction. They believed, visualized, prayed, took action, persevered, and had passion and drive towards making things happen. It took them years and perhaps even decades, but eventually the success came rolling in. They watched their business take off and skyrocket into victory.

There are those who meet someone, fall in love, and get married. Both partners had enough money coming in that enabled them to buy a house. They were in great spirits, had children, some pets, and were content with the way this was. In essence, they achieved a happy life, which equates to attracting in abundance and the law of attraction. They might not be all that spiritual. They're just living life and fighting to make things happen, because they know that sitting around dreaming will not bring in the abundance.

One of the reasons the law of attracting abundance doesn't work for everyone is people are wired differently from one another. Some are intuitive while others are logical. The way people go about life is different than someone else. This means everyone will have different results. If anything is gained with the law of attraction it is with the hopes that it can inject some enthusiasm and motivation into your aura that you can accomplish your dreams if you go out there and seize it!

Those that expose the law of attracting abundance rightly take offense to an extent. This is partially due to the fact that some in law of attraction circles have suggested or stated that someone poor or abused and living in an impoverished area brought that on themselves through the law of attraction.

They did not bring that kind of life onto themselves. They were born into it through their parents. There are also a great many success stories of people that broke out of that kind of life. They had that burning desire and dream, then worked hard to find a way to make it come true. They were motivated and self-empowered. Obtaining any measure of wealth without working for it will rarely end well. Sometimes what you desire never comes. Maybe it comes later in life after hard work and a positive attitude. Or it comes in a different form than you expected.

Another misconception of the law of attracting abundance is that if you're a happy go lucky personality who just wants everyone to love each other and have fun, then you'll attract in abundance. This is untrue, dangerous, and an outlandish request to place on human beings. Someone who has a downtrodden personality will not wake up one day of having that personality and suddenly be joyous and singing through the streets with a big smile. You're asking people to go against their personality and become someone their temperament is not in order to attract in abundance. When the truth is that a great many people have attracted in abundance by being their usual dark personality. They put in the hard work and then got lucky when the right people saw it that suddenly catapulted them to success. There is no magic in that, but luck, faith, persistence, and hard work. Besides I've encountered happy joyful personalities, but discovered there was unhappiness hidden deep down.

Positive thinking goes a long way, but so does getting off the couch and actually getting to work. That's one of the core action traits to incorporate and start off with. You need to have some measure of reality in check. It is better to believe that you can and will achieve, than to sit around waiting to die while debunking all of this positivity and goodness that the law of attraction crowd keeps feeding you about getting happy and to get moving and going. Sometimes we all need a little reminder of motivation from each other.

When you're down or having an issue you may go to a counselor or a friend to vent. When you leave them after getting it off your chest, you feel a bit better. Perhaps they said something that put you at ease. In that respect, they did their job.

People need certain people at times for that reminder. If it comes in the form of an abundance book, seminar, article, or video, then that's all that matters. Because most of the time what's discussed worked for someone out there. If you work hard and believe you will achieve, then you will fight to the ends of the earth and go as far as you can to make it happen. Sitting around with a positive aura and waiting for it to happen will not work. It is a start, but you will need to stand up and take action steps towards making it happen.

PART 2

»⧓«»⧓«»⧓«»⧓«»⧓«»⧓«»⧓«

Preparing for Abundance

»⧓«»⧓«»⧓«»⧓«»⧓«»⧓«»⧓«

CHAPTER FIVE

A Student of the Law of Attracting in Abundance

Many teach abundance attracting philosophies all over the world in books, on social media, on stage, in webinars and seminars. It's not like it was centuries ago when a student or initiate had to graduate to a certain level before being admitted into a special school that would teach these ideas only after you were ready.

The challenges and positives of this are that yes it is easily accessible to anybody that seeks it out, but the dangers are that the person may not be in a position spiritually where they are ready for that type of class. It's like a fifth grader skipping grades to attend a twelfth grade senior class. They may sit there and wonder what is all this the teacher is talking about. They haven't gradually worked their way up spiritually, emotionally, and mentally by taking the necessary steps to become fully fledged enough that they are ready to be trained in new concepts.

In the original movie, *The Karate Kid*, the young guy wanted to excel in the ways of karate. He's guided to a master teacher that ridicules him, then has him do unending chores around his house. This goes on for eons until the student loses patience. He recklessly goes off with frustration not understanding when he'll be taught what he came to learn, which is to be a master at karate. He learns the hard way that the teacher was in fact teaching him karate. The teacher was building him up to that because the teacher knew this kid was too eager and arrogant, and therefore not ready to be taught the true ways and art of karate. The kid wanted to partake in actual karate right out of the gate. He had initially been unaware that he was being trained as a karate champion by partaking in those household chores first. The teacher was testing him to see if he had what it takes. This was by making him work for it.

Some expect the rewards at their door after watching one video, one seminar or reading one book. Give me the rewards without working for it! Those that jump to the front of the line might receive the rewards, but not without a price. This payment might come in the form where the rewards are short lived and it's all ripped away. All of the gifts that poured in out of nowhere disappear because the person hadn't worked for it. They had not gone through the steady training that builds them up to that level they ultimately want to reach. They more or less rolled out of bed and started reading a law of attraction book, then automatically expected the gifts and blessings to come soaring down immediately afterwards. When it didn't happen that way they became disappointed, then took it a step further and criticized the movement and anyone that adheres to it as being gullible or naive.

When you're absorbed in the dark part of your ego that you are above doing the chores that a master teacher is giving you, then you will be more apt to walking away calling it all bogus. Hopefully, you'll receive a moment of enlightening clarity realizing you were in fact being trained and prepped for what you were seeking. In *The Karate Kid*, his physical body movements while doing these household chores were the movements the student would use that would win him the Karate championship down the line.

You are gaining tools in life through your work experiences that seem like a mundane monotonous job you do for the paycheck. You are gaining tools in life through your personal experiences in relationships with lovers and friendships. Those particular relationship friend partnerships tested and pushed you to look at things a different way. They are the ones that challenged you to change certain aspects of you that could be improved. All of this was making you smarter and sharper. The one that perseveres and does the grunt work knowing they're becoming stronger and smarter are the ones that excel and go far. You are enduring the experiences and absorbing the information that has been fed to you in this book thus far for a reason. It is priming you for what's to come and how you'll view and accept things along your Earthly life journey.

In another film scenario in, *Dangerous Minds*, the teacher gives the students a poem to learn offering that the winner will receive a prize. One student jumps the gun only interested in the rewards, "What's the prize?"

The teacher says, "Learning and understanding is the prize. Knowing how to think is the prize."

Student says, "I know how to think right now."

Teacher says, "Yeah, well you know how to run too, but not the way you could run if you trained."

A-ha.

Teacher continues, "The mind is like a muscle and if you want to be really powerful, you got to work it out. Each new fact gives you a choice. Each new idea builds another muscle. It's those muscles that are going to make you really strong. Those are your weapons, and in this unsafe world, I want to arm you."

Student asks, "And that's what these poems are supposed to do?"

Teacher says, "Hey, try it. You're just sitting here anyway. Look, okay, if at the end of the term, you're not faster, stronger, and smarter, you will have lost nothing. But if you are, you'll be that much tougher to knock down."

If you jump too quickly to get to the goal, then the rewards and the blessings will result in a disappointing outcome. If you don't have the experience and knowledge gained through good old-fashioned hard work, then the results could be mediocre or non-existent. Through the jobs you hold, you are gaining additional tools in that role you'll use later in life. Through your personal relationships with others, you are gaining lessons learned that make you stronger and smarter.

Someone can pick up a particular book in hopes of gaining knowledge they're not quite ready for. An innocent person picks up a law of attraction book only to find out that their thoughts are creating their reality. It can be too much to throw at someone not ready for it or not understanding that on a deeply powerful level. Therefore, they struggle with their thoughts and in some cases there are people who ended up in a worse state than before they read the book. Because the message is misinterpreted that one has to change their thoughts to be 100% positive or they will forever be doomed.

It may seem easy for a financially successful master teacher to tell everyone to think and feel positive, because they live in an environment conducive to a positive well-being. They have their expensive beautiful house in a calming sanctuary area. It's easy to maintain positivity with that kind of a life and environment. This is by no means knocking the teacher. On the contrary, this is about understanding the reality in front of you.

It is to understand the reality of where that teacher is and where a student might be. The discord between where both people are is super wide. You cannot jump from one point to another in a matter of seconds. You have to train rigorously and gradually in life.

All of this discussed in this chapter is the reasoning behind the extensive abundance curriculum that began with the lecture in the first section of this book. Next up we will dive into basic spirit and Divine guidance, wisdom, and messages that most anyone can adopt and apply into their daily life. This will assist in fine tuning your body, mind, and soul to become a stronger Divine conduit, which will simultaneously help crack open that door to abundance that most everyone wishes for. In the final section of the book, we'll begin the process of opening that abundance door.

CHAPTER SIX

Finding a Blissful Happy Place

*O*ne of the many general advice tips to apply to your life and begin the process of attracting in abundance is to think and speak positive words. This is preached in nearly most every spiritual or religious circle or group. Overall this wisdom might sound cliché and vaguely generic, but there is a reason this tip is so popular. There is some basis of proven truth to it. Understand the depth of the meaning of thinking, speaking, and feeling positive words. This is telling you that the majority of the time your thoughts and feelings should be on the positive side if you are intending to make a desire come true. You are thinking positive thoughts and speaking positive words whenever you can.

This isn't telling anybody that it's a crime or a sin to fall into negativity on occasion, because you will. You are a human being having a human experience that entails all of the colorful ranges of emotions and thoughts based on your current experience.

General spiritual practitioners preach that you be all love and light. If every person on the planet exuded that state, then there would no doubt be peace on Earth. Since this is not a realistic or practical request that the billions of people on the planet are capable of following, we have to examine this on a deeper realistic level. Some recipients have found they've fallen into the cracks of negativity when attempting to move into a permanent love and light state. There are people born with a naturally genuine bubbly personality, but not everyone wakes up in laughing joyful upbeat hysterics ready to seize each day in this manner. In fact, some people might even become a bit skeptical of a personality that exudes that infectious joyful state all day long, while others might say, "I'll have what that person is having."

Earth would be a blissful awesome place to reside on if every human being on the planet were able to achieve that bright, joyful, goofy, loving life state all day long. Imagine yourself walking around in that state feeling that energy essence throughout each day. It can make you feel good, and bring in more of those good vibrations to you, but that is also not a realistic practical demand to place on a human being.

Every person on the planet is having a specific human experience with trials, tribulations, challenges, coupled with varying measures of success, good times, and blessings. Everyone would love to have the latter kind of life and state of mind and being where you are filled to the brim of good feelings. Why wouldn't you? Who wants to feel a heavy weight of ugliness sitting on top of you day in and day out? It's an exhausting way to live with such a heavy burden sitting on top of your back.

Find the healthiest balance you can between making changes in your life through baby action steps that will help you achieve a more positive state. At the same time, be realistic that you will have set backs and challenges thrown at you out of nowhere that can throw your life off balance. That equation is inevitable and a part of life. Those types of rougher challenges help you grow, evolve and change.

It's also not a realistic demand to place on the masses to be joyful every second, especially for the millions of people around the world battling mental and emotional health issues and disorders. This is something that touches me on a more personal level. Some were born with that in their disposition, while others developed it over time due to traumatic life experiences. As someone who is included in that statistic of battling mental and emotional health issues, I understand how difficult it can be to keep yourself in balance. Who more appropriate to discuss this with you than someone that understands the nature of the beast by battling with that in daily life.

Bouncing around blissfully all day long is a wonderful space to reside and view circumstances in, but that's not what helps you grow and evolve. It is the hard times and the tough experiences that shape you. That is what assists in the soul's evolving process. This can be seen in the many success stories out there. When you investigate that person's past, you discover they came from some measure of abuse or trials and tribulations that seem more severe than others. They tend to appear composed, centered, and strong, with a warrior like stance.

It's inhuman and impractical to be positive and optimistic 100% of the time. Your thoughts and feelings fluctuate throughout each day depending on your mental, emotional, and physical state. The more positive you are, then the better the results. You can get by as long as the ratio of positive is larger than the negative. For example, it can be 75% positive and 25% negative, then the chances of you making a stronger matched vibrational connection with the positive flow of abundance is greater than if those numbers were reversed. If the percentage of negativity you give off is greater than the positive, then it is the negative that will expand and bring more of that to you.

If you're generally a positive person with the occasional negativity that's on the bare minimum side, then the positive quotient is strong enough to make some traction. If you're always negative or you are more negative than positive, then you'll need to work on that. The negative essence is too great and overbearing to bring in something positive. The consequences are that more negativity comes into your life. The more positivity you can conjure up, then the more likely you will be in a state of positive abundance reception.

I've witnessed those who are perpetually negative where they always seem to have one thing going wrong after another in their life. I've also observed those who are typically positive people, and they always seem to have great things going on for them. It's too consistent not to notice this pattern. Many others have noticed this design too, especially abundance preachers, which is why it's one of the hotter tips always made in abundance circles. And that is to be positive!

Being optimistic includes looking for that silver lining when in a crises. Not only does that help with the abundance attracting business process, but it also helps in re-training your mind to finding creative solutions to issues that arise in your life, rather than seeing the constant bleak hopelessness of where you are currently at today.

A major crises is expected to create upset, which is understood. It also depends on what one views a crises to be. In the latter years, any crises and drama that has taken place around me throughout the course of my life was taken in stride. When I was younger and immature, my reaction was more aggressive and erratic. That's one of the things you hope tempers with age. A legitimate major crises would be losing a loved one, but a false major crises might be ones obsession over a gossip media story that pushes you to see it as the end of the world. It's generally not the end of the world and you move onto the next gossip media story.

Many around me have commented that I seem to be the calm inside the storm or that my emotional reaction to things is on an even keel, while others might have a harder time with managing dramatic curve balls thrown at them. Their stress, anger, and upset will shoot from 0-100 in the span of five seconds. Others will skyrocket past that as you may likely recall seeing them in hysterics making all kinds of noise.

You might also be aware and conscious enough to notice some that rise in anger and upset tantrum energy. They are catapulted into the sphere of creating a domino effect of negative circumstances into their life preceding that. When you then look at those that reveal a calmer demeanor while in crises, you may note how strong and in control they are over an issue. Circumstances tend to go much smoother for those personality types. They also make exceptional leaders who can take care of emergencies as swiftly as a Fireman answering a bell. Obviously the latter tend to be people that are destined trailblazers.

A great leader has calm strong composure most of the time, like my 15th second cousin, Queen Elizabeth I, who also shared my life path number 1 for those numerology lovers. When the life path number 1 is showcasing the best parts of themselves, they are ordained to lead in some way.

Human beings were designed to be a fully-fledged thinking feeling consciousness. We get moody, stressed, upset, depressed and on and on. This isn't about denying those feelings and thoughts when you move into that space. Feel your feelings, think your thoughts, and be aware and mindful of them. Don't feel guilty about experiencing rough feelings. This is about having the additional awareness of everything that is happening around you. This helps in being completely conscious of when you've hit a negative state. Look at what can be done about it. Examine what caused it and what you can do to remedy it.

Don't fake positivity if you're not feeling that. Avoid kicking or beating yourself up if you find it impossible to pretend to be happy if that's not your current disposition. It takes time to work on becoming more of an optimistic positive person. Cut yourself some slack and focus on working on being more aware of your overall thoughts and feelings. If it's always negative, then work on attempting to shift that into something positive at least once a day if even for a few minutes at a time. The more you put that into practice, the easier it gets before you find it happens effortlessly and naturally.

When you're asked to be positive and optimistic, this also means that you need to be more positive than negative. This is cutting you some slack and giving you a bit of leeway to be negative on occasion. This doesn't mean be negative deliberately because you're allowed.

This would apply to those who are told, "You're too negative."

They're response is, "I don't care, I'm mad and they all need to know."

Do they really need to know or is your ego bruised about something? The Devil works in mysterious ways as God does. The Darkness ensures you remain stuck in a negative state. The Darkness part of the Devil is not to be confused with the Dark that some light spirits reside in because they understand it well. Statistics have revealed that a higher number of people believe in the possibility of God, but a far lower number believe in the possibility of the Devil. How can one witness the dark demonic behavior of humankind day after day and not suspect that there is a something more sinister interfering? The sinister energy comes from within the Darkness of ego that resides in each human soul.

When you fall into negativity, then recognize when you have. Work on improving that state again without guilt of having fallen into a downtrodden state, since guilt can lower your vibration. Your overall demeanor is content and at peace, with the occasional hiccups that come in here and there. Involve prayer, meditation, and quiet retreats into your life. You can do this anywhere that helps you move into a more serene state, such as at home in a private space or go to a quiet nature locale.

You can get to an optimistic space easier if you take a step back to acknowledge the positive things you're grateful for in your life today. You can move closer in that direction if you focus on hobbies and activities that make you smile, rather than doing things that aggravate your natural centered state of being.

Acknowledge the blessings you have today that may sometimes be taken for granted until it's taken away. Are you able to live in the place you currently live in comfortably knowing your bills are getting paid? Then that's something to be grateful for. You're not on the streets with nowhere to go and no one to turn to. Do you have a car or a mode of transportation to get you to work and other places you need to go to? That's another blessing.

Make a list of the things you're grateful for in your life today. Type it out in an email to yourself. The benefit of that is it helps you to take a few minutes to think about the things that are working in your life. If it's something that seems insignificant, write it down anyway. As you're writing it out, you're taking that moment to acknowledge its existence through focus while marinating in that thought and feeling of gratitude. You start to feel a bit better in the process. You might even have that moment of clarity, "Wow, I guess I do have some things that are working. Never really thought about that."

It's human nature to constantly seek out and obtain things. You obtain one thing, then you're quickly onto the next. This is followed by disregarding what you just achieved instead of taking that extra moment to realize how grateful and blessed you are in that moment for obtaining what you originally sought out.

I thank God and my Spirit team daily for the

blessings that come into my life. If I need assistance with something or someone, I will request it in prayer. Once it pans out well, I quickly thank my team. I've said things like, "I don't want you to think I don't acknowledge what just took place. I am highly aware of how you've just helped me with this and I thank you. Thank you for putting up with me and for helping me with this."

Because I know what a pain I can be at times, even though from spirits perspective, they are unfazed about that.

You can have whatever it is you desire, pending it is aligned with your higher self. You are a master magician able to create all of the wonders you've always longed for right there in your mind. This is the first place that the manifestation process begins. What an amazing power you have to be able to access all of that right within you. You don't need any divination tools, nor do you need to recite any special invocations, unless that's something you enjoy doing, but in the end it's not necessary. Move the thoughts in your mind right into your spirit. Use those psychic clair sense channels you have built into you since the birth of your soul that allows you to have a direct communication line with Heaven any time, day, or place. God gave this to you so that you can access Him whenever you like. It's like a good parent that gives you a phone line to them whenever you want or need it.

Feeling positive and optimistic means not only are you thinking and speaking positivity and radiating optimism, but you are also feeling positive and optimistic. You feel this energy essence all throughout your body, mind, and soul. Feel and experience God's white light energy throughout your body now. This means allowing yourself to feel it within and around you and your aura. This uplifting positive white light energy is rising from the Earth's ground, through your entire being and spreading throughout all your senses. It expands to ten feet, then twenty and thirty feet around you. You feel this on a massive level as it blasts out of you and upwards making a solid connection with God and with Heaven.

Imagine this light clearing away anything considered negative or toxic. This abundant uplifting optimism moves through your physical body. It penetrates your mind awakening it. Your perception grows to become more transcendent and deeper than you've ever experienced. Your spirit and soul are blasted with white light raising your vibration into the Heavens. You have now moved into the realms of becoming a powerful positive manifester!

CHAPTER SEVEN

Emotional Healing

When seeking to convey optimistic positivity, it cannot be a forced fake positivity as that energy is picked up on as negative. It's like putting a band-aid over a cut. The cut is still there as an open wound, but hidden underneath the band-aid. Your fake positivity is the cut covered by a band-aid. The Universe and Heaven know your general state even if you try and fake it. You cannot get away with a lie or hide anything from any being in Heaven. They all know what you are hiding underneath the essence of that energy. What you do, say, feel, or think is in plain view to them. This is the case even if your actions are different than how or what you feel or think.

Sometimes you can be putting on the happy face, when deep down you're miserable. You may not even be conscious of doing that. If you realize you have been conveying a fake positivity where you show the world your optimism, but deep down you're hurting or in some kind of mental or emotional pain, then that is the first step towards recovery. You've admitted you're battling while putting on that smile to others.

There are those great lyrics in that classic rock song, *Tracks of my Tears*, by Linda Ronstadt. She sang or said it best, *"People say I'm the life of the party, because I tell a joke or two. Although I might be laughing loud and hearty, deep inside I'm blue. So take a good look at my face. You know my smile looks out of place. If you look closer it's easy to trace the tracks of my tears."*

If someone you were in love with rejected or left you, then it is absurd to assume you're going to bounce back an hour after they left and dive right back into life like it never happened, unless you are a gifted sociopath with no emotions. You're going to feel the gamut of challenging feelings that may last one week or it could last one year. For some it may be even longer than that depending on how attached to the person you were. I've witnessed cases where someone never truly bounces back after that. They are forever shaped and molded a different way than they had started out due to the traumatic experience.

You would understandably experience upset, hurt, and sadness over something like that. You are unable to pull through and want to stay in bed all day. Even when you push yourself to get outside and continue to live, you experience the kind of pain that feels as if something important was ripped out of you. I've been there too for every serious love relationship that ended.

To shift that wide discord you move through the many emotional stages one experiences with something like that. Take your time, allow yourself to process it, and make sense of what's happened. Move through the various stages of grief in your own personal way that ranges from depression and sadness, to anger and rage. You'll hopefully talk about it with a friend, a counselor, or anyone that will listen. You can also write your feelings down in a word document, journal, or an email to yourself and file it away. This is to help get it out of you. Eventually you move out of those challenging emotions as you take your time processing each one.

The healing process concludes when you are able to move past those negative feeling emotions and into a state where you are willing and ready to accept and release the person that has hurt you. When you release that person, then you do it with love. Meaning there is no additional pain or malice in your heart for them. You're not condoning any bad behavior they might have done, but you are kicking out any pain that attached itself to you out of your vicinity. You no longer need it. Abuse done to you is not your fault. If you instigated something, then apologize to the person and forgive yourself for the ill will you might have caused, then release it and let it go. You don't want to carry that pain around indefinitely.

Work on getting yourself into that place where you will positively be better off without that person that caused you pain. You mentally thank them for the experience, "I bless you on your path." And then you release it and let it go.

There is no time limit as to how long it can take when it comes to moving through a healing process. This can be healing over anything, such as any kind of hurt or upset in your life, regardless of what it is. For some people it can take weeks or months, and others it may take years. There are cases where some get stuck in that cycle of hurt that lasts indefinitely for years and sometimes decades if not treated or healed. The tragedy with the latter is they remain in the exact same space they were when the initial upset happened. Sometimes you may not even be aware that you're still stuck in a cycle due to something from the past.

An example might be someone who was married for decades, then an affair breaks up the marriage. This is followed by Divorce and all of the stresses that come out of that. The person cheated on might carry the cheater in their aura until they release it. It is understandable that one would be upset by this kind of abrupt life circumstance that throws you a hard right punch, but you don't want to let it stay with you for too long. The longer it stays with you, the longer it becomes a part of you. It has the danger of shaping you into someone you might not want to become.

Where it gets exceptionally tricky is when the pain endures for years. The person never quite bounces back into life again. They just go through the motions numbed to everyone and everything around them. They become inaccessible for the right new partner or circumstance to come into their life. It also blocks the flow of abundance from coming in.

I understand all this well also having been through that in personal experiences. Years in I've hardened and become even more difficult to get close to. Through my connections with God, I begin to see it all unravel before me. I receive that high awareness I hadn't noticed before. I mentally went back into time to try and find out when I changed or was changing. Nine times out of ten, I wind up tracing it back to some kind of traumatic experience, such as a love relationship break up or childhood abuse.

In one of my earlier books, "*Reaching for the Warrior Within*", I've discussed the importance of taking those moments throughout your life to do a thorough life review. This has so many benefits that include going backwards into time to make note of the significant life circumstances that took place in your life, whether good or bad. Make note of what transpired out of that. How it might have changed you for better or worse. The worst is not about judging you. It's making amends for what changed certain traits that you're not particularly fond of, but you don't know how to change it. Acknowledging it is an important step towards changing it. You cannot change something you're unaware of.

Many years have passed after you emotionally shut down following a traumatic event, crises, or break up. You may one day awaken to realize that you had been stagnant for so long and are not sure why. This is because the incident that kicked that off was so long ago by that point, but your overall nature, personality, and demeanor had permanently changed to who you've become today. It's only when you stop to ponder and re-trace your steps backwards when you realize that who you are today was kicked off by traumatic events years prior. You had long forgotten about it, but it had also shifted your behavior patterns in the process to who you've become now. This is that moment of awakening and clarity or as some say, "A-ha! Wow, I can't believe how drastically that situation changed me. I need to do something about this today!" The process of positive change then begins at that moment you gained clarity and awareness.

You've admitted there's a problem rumbling within you. What a fantastic awareness level to reach and achieve. Because now you can begin the steps to work on healing those open wounds that caused you to deny your feelings and prevented you from moving forward and onward with life. You want to attract in a positive abundant feeling, but you wrestle with that due to the hard life circumstances that have thrown you one curve ball after another.

Heal emotional wounds through awareness, putting in the daily work, and bringing in a counselor, healer, or therapist if you're able to. If that's not feasible for any reason such as financial, seek out groups online that share your difficulties. Having camaraderie support or others to talk to that are going through a similar circumstance has more of a positive than challenging effect. The positive effect is this can empower the both of you to stand tall and up into your own. It produces healing in a quicker way than if you didn't have that support.

The challenging side can be if neither party are interested in healing and just want to rehash past circumstances for months and years longer than necessary that it turns into gossip and vengeful thoughts. This leaves you stuck in that dark state. If you've sought out help, then that means you've already surpassed the first step of being aware that you are wrestling with something difficult. Deep down you want it to stop and are ready for help. You begin the process of seeking out that assistance. You have the intention and desire to do what you can to help you through a negative chapter in your life.

I personally turn directly to God for answers and assistance. Daily prayer is always recommended to add to the equation towards healing. Ask God to work through you and to help you heal and guide you towards steps on how to do that. Request that you be helped to understand what it is you need, and to assist you in taking notice of when He is helping. Ask that He help you understand by putting that assistance in your path.

There are times that God and spirit are putting

helpful signs in front of you, but when you're wallowing in a negative state you might not notice it, since a negative state can block Divine communication. Fear not, since He is always with you and will continue to put that help in front of you indefinitely until you notice it. You will wake up one day and get that bright idea that puts you into action mode. When the answer appears it feels like it had always been there, but you hadn't noticed it until that moment.

Your emotional healing may leave a scar the way a deep cut on your body can. The wound is healed enough that it makes you whole again. "Whole again" is the perfect exceptional state you were in upon birth.

I've talked to people who have massive anger issues. They admit it's caused a ton of problems in their life, but they cannot control it. Admitting you have a problem is one of the best first steps you can take that will adjust your soul and body down the path of beautiful magnificent recovery. What an amazing gift that is to be blessed with knowingness.

Have it in your mind that you want to do the work in order to make your peace with any ill will you might have caused another person or what someone else might have caused you. This is regardless if it was you causing pain for another person or you were just cruel to yourself. You can be cruel to yourself through self-hate by your actions, thoughts, words, and feelings. You can be cruel to yourself with the addictions and toxins you continuously put into your body knowing it can result in harm. You can be cruel to yourself by saying yes to things that deep down don't feel right to you. Learning to tell others no is also a purpose some need to learn this lifetime. Naturally, there are circumstances where you do have to suck it up and say yes, such as if it is a part of your job you get paid for. This isn't about that, but about the things that morally and spiritually affect you in a negative way where you can truly say no. Your boss needs you to fax something, well of course you do that. A friend or someone that doesn't pay you keeps asking you to do something you're uncomfortable with. Saying no to that is not being rude or unaccommodating. Saying no is saying yes to you.

This illustration is important because it has an effect on your overall well-being as well as the process of positive manifestation and abundance attracting. If you remain in a negative cycle, then this will leave your life trajectory on pause for as long as it takes before you begin moving out of that state.

This applies to whatever upsetting traumatic circumstance has taken place in your life. You want to work on moving through those emotional changes associated with the experience while eventually reaching a place where you can release it. This isn't just to benefit you, your body, mind, and soul, but it also assists in helping you to continue on living this life you've been blessed with. Bad experiences happen on some level for everyone, even the most seemingly privileged person. No one is exempt from enduring some form of rock and roll in their life.

Experiences both good and bad are designed to

teach you lessons that positively affect your soul's growth process. The higher level your soul reaches, the greater the abundant attraction quotient is. Abundance being about your overall state of mind, rather than financial increase. The desire for riches is a hollow goal that does not fulfill in the end. Having enough income coming in can certainly bring you less stress in your life to one extent. This is in the ways that it would allow you to quit a soul crushing day job and dive into work that is your passion and life purpose. The income gained should be used to continue improving your soul while giving you more time and energy to apply towards your passionate soul driven life purpose work that helps others.

You may be perfectly content today, even though you might have endured traumatic experiences earlier in life, such as in childhood, but if you have not made your peace with what happened to you in an earlier part of your life, then you are subconsciously carrying that around with you even if you've suppressed it. This also has an effect on your manifestation process today.

If you're attempting to examine your life today to see what could be blocking the positive flow of abundance and none is evident, then move further back into time to see what wounds have yet to be healed. Sometimes journaling, writing about it, or talking about it can help get it out of you to make your peace with it. Another additional way is to find a comfortable spot in a nature setting or a private space at home to commune with God regularly. Even though you can conduct prayer anywhere you like from walking to your car, sitting in traffic, or while you're getting ready for the day. The benefit of finding a space to have an in-depth prayer session is that it helps you be distraction free in order to fully focus on any guidance that is coming in. Ask Heaven what needs to be healed in your life. This can include old forgotten wounds that are still present in your subconscious. This will help increase the flow of positive abundance energy.

CHAPTER EIGHT

Gratitude and Optimism

Gratitude is one of the greater ways to increase bounty in your life. This is not fake appreciation with the hidden goal of obtaining increase, since Heaven knows when you're being deceptive. It has to be a genuine gratitude where you truly do feel this gratitude within every cell of your being. Gratitude is a challenging trait to display because the darkness of ego part of someone desires to be thankless preferring to be greedy. In America, on Thanksgiving the tradition is everyone gives thanks and gratitude to those around them. The irony is the next day is Black

Friday, one of the larger shopping days of the year causing a rise in greed and violence.

Be grateful for what you have in your life here and now. Living in a miserable or pessimistic state blocks the flow of abundance and increases the challenges in your life due to God's law of the universe.

You could be struggling in life and facing insurmountable challenges, but everyone is battling something. Some of those challenges they're battling with could be considered as being worse than someone else's depending on whom you ask. Any form of uncomfortable struggle still counts as energy in the eyes of the Universe.

This isn't telling you not to fall into pessimism or negativity, because everyone has some measure of struggle. Even the most optimistic person will experience some browbeaten feelings and thoughts. No one is exempt from challenges. This is just explaining what can block the flow of positive abundance.

All energy expands regardless of the tone of that energy. If you're positive, then this positive energy will expand. If it's negative, then that's what will expand and bring more of that to you. Since this is deemed the case, functioning in an optimistic state when it is possible will have more benefit than not.

Don't force positivity if you're not feeling it. Avoid beating yourself up if you're battling negatively. Take your time being aware of the moments you're in a negative state. Look at what is causing it, then examine what action steps you can take to relieve that stress. If you are unable to do anything about it, then work on letting it go.

You could be sitting in daily traffic that doesn't move, which always angers and upsets you. Sitting in your car in upset will not lighten the traffic. It also won't help in getting to your destination quicker. All it does is attack your soul and pull you down. You arrive at your location stressed and edgy. When you look at the detrimental effects it places on your back, then it's easier to move out of that, because you mentally say, "I don't want to live in misery either. I need to shake this off. God please help me move out of this stress and back into joy. And so it is."

When I've been in those situations I've worked extra hard to move my angry stressed thoughts into something more productive. Use that time to mentally communicate to God and your Spirit team to help alleviate the stress you continue to feel over circumstances you cannot do anything about. In addition, ask for Divine help in mending the areas that you are able to. Ask God for help and to put ideas in your mind that you can take action on to fix a situation you'd like to see positive changes with.

It can be easy to fall into a state of pessimism when nothing good is going for you, but if you're breathing and you're alive, then that's something to be grateful for. Do you have a place to lay your head, food on the table, clothing, and the basic practical survival necessities needed? Then that's something to be grateful for. Imagine having one or all of that taken away with no one to turn to, because this has happened to a great number of people all across history. How would you feel if that happened?

Statistics have revealed that over 70% of people despise their job. Many people rightly complain about their job, especially if you're working in an abusive environment with toxic people. It could be a soul crushing job that kills off your life force. You could work with one or more difficult people. You partake in work that doesn't inspire you to want to do it, but you do it for the paycheck to survive. You're not doing work that makes you passionate. When you move back into gratitude, you're able to observe the job from a higher perspective. The more challenging plight is when the job is toxic or abusive. Pray daily for a way out into something better and more improved.

Otherwise say, "I know I sometimes complain about my job, and I do want to make a positive job change, but at the same time I am grateful that I have a paycheck coming in. I know if I didn't have that, then who knows what would happen. In that respect, I am grateful for this job. I'll do my best to look at it positively while I'm there until I can find another change I can make to move out of that."

State that kind of an affirmation by not just saying the words, but realize how the words ring true. Feel the gratitude that you have this job and are genuinely blessed. Through that move you are raising your vibration again. The vibration is being raised to match the level of the type of abundance you wish to attract into your life. You are the magnet and the abundance is the steel. You are drawing it to you or away from you depending on your actions, thoughts, and feelings of every moment of every day.

Heaven and the Universe, which we use interchangeably, ensure your basic needs are met. They help with what you need, not always necessarily with what you want, especially if what you want is not beneficial for your higher self. If they do see that it will benefit your growth and higher self, then they will work with you to help bring that which you desire to fruition. All potential and possible factors would need to be examined for each person.

There are various time delays per person as to when particular blessings are bestowed on that soul. Each person's trajectory is different from another person's. It's not that one person is more worthy of blessings over another soul. There are various factors that have to come into play as to what is delaying blessings and miracles.

For every soul on Earth, the desire for blessings and miracles have many factors which come into play to determine whether they will be granted. For someone in the United States, they may have a middle class somewhat comfortable lifestyle as opposed to someone born in a country or area where restrictions, suffocation, bondage, and resistance are evident. There are third world countries where people live in inadequate and unsafe conditions. They may never know what it's like to be able to manifest what you desire.

At the same time, many are brought up in these conditions where they know no other way. They may not have television or internet and have no idea of what is happening in other parts of the world. They may be perfectly content because it is all they know. They weren't brought up in a country or city that displays a desire for excess in front of them around the clock. What they choose to desire may not be as high as what someone else desires in a wealthier city.

The person in a Third World Country may desire to attract in enough food for one night's dinner. Whereas in another part of the world, that wealthy person is bombarded with imagery that you can be whatever you want to be and achieve whatever you want to achieve if you set your mind to it. Maybe you will, but will that bring you ultimate happiness?

Ultimate happiness is the state of high personal soul power. It's climbing beyond the superficiality and the physical to achieve an absolute transcending spiritual life force.

The positive side effect to that utopia reached is other physical manifestations and abundance. Many that reach a higher soul spiritual level no longer desire materialistic excess. This is not limited to the basic human survival needs of a home, food, and clothing. Add to that good friends or a loyal loving love partner, pending you desire the latter. Some spiritual soul achievers tend to be perfectly comfortable alone.

Sometimes it can be that you are indeed ready for blessings. You've done the hard work and experienced what you were intended to in order to bring you to the place you're at today. You have consistently maintained this hard work ethic, but still nothing has transpired to help you have that breakthrough you've long desired. You've done everything right, but nothing has come to pass. In those cases, there are other elements at play preventing the blessings from coming in.

It can be your Spirit team is working diligently behind the scenes with you, but there are free will choice delays that have taken place. It can be that those who are intended to notice your hard work are not paying attention to it, even though the signs have been in front of them forever. Other times it can be that you're doing everything right, but you express no gratitude. Complaining into abundance doesn't work. It just tells the universe bring me this thing I don't want as fast as you can. All it does is reverse the positive manifestation process.

Work on being grateful for what you have now. Being ungrateful will block and delay what you desire. It's that negative energy that stalls forward movement. It's understandable to feel frustrated when you've been doing the hard work for so long and yet nothing has come to assist and give you that big miracle breakthrough you long for. It's not like you're being punished and the Universe is purposely withholding blessings from you while granting it to others that you feel are less deserving of it. Feeling envy blocks the flow of abundance. It's also not anyone's place to decide who is worthy of what and when. There are varying time limits for each person that determine when and if abundance will flow in and what that will entail.

You're going to feel negative feelings on occasion in terms of what is or isn't coming in. You'll feel frustrated and envious of others that seem to get blessed instantly. This is about recognizing when those feelings hit you and working quickly to eradicate it and move back into a positive alignment. It takes practice and discipline to re-train your mind into a new way of thinking and seeing things. Changing your ways will not drastically happen overnight. It's a gradual methodical process that will take work and focus on your part.

Whenever you notice anything good happening in your life, whether or not it's big or small, remember to say daily, "I Am Blessed!"

You are blessed in the smallest of details, the smallest of ways, there is that glimmer of light that attempts to crack its way in to help you remember to believe again. If you're interested in attracting in positive abundance, then be genuinely grateful for what you have now.

CHAPTER NINE

Complaining Into Abundance

*I*n an earlier chapter, we talked about how others have expressed disdain over the belief that is thrust upon people regarding the law of attraction that demands you be positive to attract in abundance. This is not something my Spirit team preaches and demands, because you will experience negativity on occasion. It's not insisted that you be positive every single second, since that is not realistic or practical for a human being. It is about being mindful and aware of your overall state of mind in general. This means that as long as you're more positive and optimistic, than negatively stressed, depressed, and angry, then the positive quotient is high enough to pull in positive abundance. You're in the clear if most of the time you're a fairly positive and optimistic person.

The dangers of pretending to be positive when deep down you're not is that the Universe looks at how you're feeling. You could put on the façade that you're optimistic and positive, but if what you're feeling underneath is struggle and negativity, then that is what the Universe pulls in because that is the overall nature you're conveying, not the deceptive face on the exterior, but your entire energetic being state.

Some have said, "I'm not naïve for being positive and optimistic. I just choose to look at the bright side of things."

This is a fantastic mantra to have as long as you're not falling into denial over an abusive situation that's taken place. This is also pending that what you're being optimistic about is aligned with God's will for your soul in the end. Looking to have your ego stroked or having a distorted excited goal of being popular is not aligned with the Light. It's losing your way and falling into the deception of the Darkness.

Deception is not going to be obvious, which is why it's called deception. Deception shows up as something that can easily entice and lure you into its trap. It has to be something or someone attractive enough that it causes you to light up with excitement. This is the danger of deception, because it shows up in this attractive form pulling you in until you later realize, "Wow! I've been had. How did I not see this?"

It's because the Darkness shows up in this way. Its goal is to pull you in and drown you in it. You later realize after much time has passed that you got sucked into something that had deceived you. This can apply to anything such as when someone promises you all sorts of stuff that never pans out. You find out you wasted hundreds or thousands of dollars on something pointless that had no positive benefit.

Deception can show up as a hot looking guy or girl you find attractive. You become blinded by their beauty bending over backwards to cater to their every whim. One day you wake up and realize it was always you being the giver. They were consistently taking advantage of that by receiving and never giving. You obtained a temporary rushed high from the object of your desires positive reaction over what they received from you that you continue to keep giving and giving. That is until you hopefully wake up and realize that there is a grave imbalance in the connection. You could discover they were never truly that interested in you, but couldn't say no to the constant kindness you kept bestowing on them. This is how one gets taken advantage of, which can also lead you to feel resentment.

This is why it's called deception, because deception is not going to show up as deception. It's going to show up as something attractive enough to lure you in and pull you down. It's designed to trick and deceive you into falling for it.

When you discover you were deceived, then you look upon it as if you had been out of your mind while the deception took place.

A positive person can fall into despair every now and then, but it is not their permanent daily state. If you're complaining every single day about the same issues for months on end, and there is no positive change, then take a look at that.

There is no doubt that on my journey towards accomplishing what I wanted to, there were moments I ignored my Spirit team's guidance and fell prey to the allure of the darkness convincing me that I will never obtain what I seek. In younger naïve days, I have been led astray down a different path that looked like it was filled with glitter, but wound up full of deception. I've also fallen into daily complaining about an issue until I receive that eye opener. It prompts me to say, "I'm starting to annoy myself. I need to stop this at once. How did I allow this to endure for so long?"

You're suddenly sounding like a broken record at that point, even to yourself.

Complaining is an abundance and increase killer. When you're in tune, aware, and conscious of what's happening around you, then are also more in tune to picking up on how complaining can make you feel. It doesn't feel good, it lowers your vibration, and you feel this ugly weight on you afterwards. This isn't telling you to never complain as everybody whines on some level. This also isn't saying that there isn't anything to complain about. You could easily find at least one thing to complain about daily.

The moments I'm alone, productive, and working, there are no complaints filtering through my mind. When I'm with a fun positive uplifting friend, there are no complaints moving through either of us, so it can be done. It doesn't even cross our minds. It's only when certain personalities come around that it moves it into a complaint, then I find I've become caught in its web if it continues indefinitely. Find people that tend to move into positivity to connect with.

Generally, it's other people that can infect your aura, specifically the gossipy complaining ones. Sometimes it's just good humor and harmless, but other times it's bathed in hostility. You likely know that one person in your life where everytime you bump into them they are harshly complaining about something. If you're a clairsentient sensitive empath type, then you can feel your entire body shift, stress, and tense up. You walk away from that person feeling low. When before you encountered them you were doing great and riding on cloud nine.

There is also that one friend you may know of that everytime you bump into them there is some kind of gossip. They see you and shout, "There you are! You are not going to believe what I just found out about Karen."

No one needs to hear about the gossip you've dug up on Karen. Worry about your own life and work on fixing that, because generally if someone's life is that dull, they will negatively fixate on other people's lives. The obsession some personality types have for gossip is also what made the tabloid industry a billion dollar enterprise. They have enough people wanting to follow the lives of the rich and famous. Buying tabloids or frequenting gossip sites is not usually to get inspired, but to either falsely worship a celebrity you don't personally know or harshly criticize them. Neither does well to open the floodgates to attracting in abundance. This is due to the energy involved with gossip and complaining about them.

Everyone complains on some level, which usually comes from the inner feelings experienced. I feel this, I feel that, I feel I feel. Feelings are the culprit for a great deal of unhappiness. It drives one to an addiction. Some complain about their jobs, others complain about the daily traffic, some complain about their friends, family members, lovers or a situation that happened while out at a store.

Become self-aware and mindful of what you're complaining about. Is complaining about it helping to resolve an issue, or is it just splattering negative gossip energy around? Notice how you feel when you're complaining as it's happening. It may give some people a rushed high at first, but like sugar or alcohol, you inevitably feel that low drop in energy causing you to crash to the floor. If it's continuously bringing your energy down when you're done venting, then work to untangle from that and let whatever it is bothering you go.

Choose your battles wisely. What situations can use your warrior like vigilance in correcting and what can you foresee as being a complete waste of time.

Sometimes it helps to complain about something with someone in order to come to a resolution. You're having relationship issues and don't know what to do about it. When you have the goal of wanting to correct the issue, then complaining can be temporarily warranted. Talking it out with someone can help you come to a resolve that will work. Complaining wanders along that fine line of helpful to toxic. Is the complaining constructive in order to reach a positive resolution? Or is the complaining taking place because you're dying to harshly trash someone because you hate that they're doing well in life while you've been struggling? The latter is non-productive for you since it's not hurting or harming the target, but your own well-being. This is part of taking care of you, so that you can stay on track and on path towards accomplishing your ultimate goals in life. This is whether spiritually, emotionally, mentally, or physically.

Humanity would be a step closer to a Utopian world if everyone would stop ranting and raving about. The repeat offenders don't know to stop and are unable to get over whatever they're constantly angry about. Some of the largest complaining noise happens on social media, which is often used as a public diary to air your venting about what happened when you were trying to get into a parking space at the grocery store.

You likely know there are social media accounts that are filled to the brim of some kind of non-constructive rant about someone or something they despise. This isn't about the occasional slip that an overall positive person falls into where they suddenly take a moment to complain about something. This is about the regular offenders where the majority of their posts are negatively based every hour of every day. It doesn't do anything to help matters. It certainly doesn't contribute to bringing more love into the world. Someone looking to bring more love into the world already knows this won't help their causes.

There are now statistics and scholar studies surrounding the negative effects of social media with sites like Twitter. Twitter has grown to be a platform for predominately negative energy rather than positivity. There is also growing evidence that it contributes to increasing anxiety and depression symptoms.

There is something eerie about having an unqualified suspect tweeting out something that can negatively destroy someone's well-being by accusing them of a crime they never partook in. This is how dangerous social media has become. Those guilty of it don't feel they're contributing anything negative. When you're buried that deep into it, it's difficult to see clearly. This is why gossip is considered one of the toxic addictions and part of the deadly sins. This is due to the array of negative issues it causes both to the sender and any recipient. The darkness wins by using the naïve and guilty as his pawn towards humanities destruction and downfall.

The limitless statistics repeatedly popping up cite and illustrate that many people are finding this to be a growing problem. I also hear from many people informing me they're shutting their social media accounts down due to this happening, because it is an epidemic. There are the usual offenders that you know will quickly jump on board with every single daily top trending story that exists. Some of them have hundreds of thousands and millions of followers that bow down to their every word. It's like the pied piper leading them all to slaughter.

There are moments I've fallen into a complaint, but I'm fully aware of it. I've said, "Okay I need to wrap this up and move on, because I'm just irritating myself now."

Dwelling in that kind of toxicity doesn't help anything. Release any anger and resentment you have towards whoever or whatever it is you're complaining about. Let it go because you don't need it. Carrying the pain or heaviness of the complaining energy is not harming the target of your complaint. It is just a toxicity festering inside you that has been scientifically proven to manifest into health issues down the line.

Can you not feel that energy while in the gossip complaint? Are you not tired of living like that? You don't need to carry the unnecessary pain. Give it away to Heaven to transmute and turn it into gold.

Do you complain about having no money? What action steps can you do to change that? If the answer is nothing, then that's an action step you're choosing to make. Making no move is making a move.

If your thoughts are filled with negative talk, you

may as well work on shifting that to something positive. Since you have thoughts racing in your mind as it is, wouldn't you rather listen to good stuff than bad? No one is forcing you to think a certain way. You have control over what you're thinking. That's one of the things you actually do have control over. You can spend your life regurgitating negative things about yourself, or you can begin the process of adopting more positive things to say about yourself. No one else can control that except you. Look at the good you have now, because you have more good in you than you realize or are willing to admit or notice.

I'm not immune to the occasional negative thoughts and feelings either. It was much more prevalent when I was younger, but as I grew older I learned to stand into my own and appreciate the good aspects of me. It wasn't an overnight change of course, but a gradual one as I put this into practice. I don't remember my negative self-talk being particularly severe or damaging. It wasn't as bad as the words my deceased father said to me growing up that had more of a permanent psychological impact. Ironically, I was particularly loving and supportive towards myself, which no doubt was coming from God.

My motto as a teenager was that if no one will support me, then I will support myself. That still holds true today. By the time I was sixteen, I knew that if I was going to survive on this physical plane that I better find a job. My family was poor and we grew up with no money, so I knew the only way to not allow that to continue was to fight to make it on my own. I ended up doing that successfully. I prayed, connected to God and my team daily, and followed their action steps. They showed me one thing, I accomplished it, then they showed me another, and I accomplished that, and so on. This is how God works. You'll continuously be shown the same thing for days, weeks, months, and even years until you finally notice the synchronicity to make that move. You delay that move out of fear or by not realizing that it was a psychic hit from Heaven.

I've heard from others who informed me of their day-to-day negative self-talk that is more along the lines of self-cruelty. Mine was more along the lines of, "Why did I say that to that person?" Or "Now why did I do that?"

I would acknowledge that for a second, but then move on from it and onto other things quickly. It doesn't mean I'm perfection, far from it, but I do my best to be aware and mindful of those moments that any negative feeling or thought I've conjured up isn't real. I realized that most of those feelings and thoughts were ultimately not based in reality, but my own personal human perception.

Imagine spending your days saying sentences like, "I have no talents, I'm not good at anything, no one likes me the way they love others, I'm unlovable, I'm hideous, why would anyone hire me, why would anyone want to be with me, I'm useless, I can't do anything right, I'll never amount to anything, I have nothing to be grateful for, my life sucks, it's always one thing after another going wrong, I'm too young, I'm too old, I'm too fat, I'm too thin...."

That must have annoyed or brought you down to read as much as it jarred me to write it. As an ever-inquisitive bee having communicated with so many people over the years I've discovered that everyone has those negative thoughts about themselves to one extent or another. For some it only enters their mind once in awhile, and for others it's a constant daily attack of badgering of themselves. Their perception of themselves is negatively skewed.

Where can it get you to sit around all day thinking low thoughts one after the other? Love yourself because you are created in His image. You were born out of Love from the creator who loves you unconditionally. Those negative words you tell yourself are untrue. They seem or feel true from your own current reality and perception, but not in the eyes of God. Not in the eyes of those in Heaven. Your soul is perfection in every way loved unconditionally for all that you are, including your strengths and what you consider to be personal flaws. Love, accept, and appreciate you, because you're a gift!

CHAPTER TEN

Stand In Your Glorious Power

When someone shouts their accomplishments from the highest mountain, then it isn't long before a negative beaten person will feel low, envy, or disdain about that. This pushes them to complain that the other person is conceited or a narcissus, instead of admiring that confident quality in that person. Use others accomplishments to motivate you to rise into who your soul is and shout that from the rooftops, rather than trying to spin it into something negative. That reaction typically comes from jealousy and envy that is buried deep in your subconscious.

Envy is one of the deadly sins for a reason. It pulls you under where the Darkness takes over, envelopes, and suffocates you in that envy. Sometimes it might be due to jealousy, other times someone isn't jealous, but just a miserable person in general. They find fault with everyone and everything. No matter the context, jealousy and envy are abundance blocks, since any form of negative emotion, feeling, or thought creates a block.

There is also the other kind of envy you may know about. This is where you're not a bad person, but you have been working so hard in life, and you're not seeing any positive results, traction, or movement. Then you see someone else do what you had been doing for years and they shoot upwards across the map. You notice something like that and it ends up created envy in you. You feel beaten down by it. Your work is exceptional, you're gifted, accomplished at what you do, and you work so hard. Then you see someone with little experience, or whom you might feel is not qualified necessarily, but they put something out and it attracts in the massive abundance. That will kick anyone on the sidelines wondering, "I don't get it. When is it my turn? I've been doing this for much longer."

Know that in those moments there isn't anything you did to attract that. Everyone has a different timeline as to when things pan out the way they're supposed to. It's important to do your best and stand strong. Say, "I am just as qualified as that person is. I'm glad that God has blessed them, and by the way I'm in that line too!"

This is also why I've forever protested to love those rags to riches stories in books, films, or music. *Erin Brockovich* with Julia Roberts is one of my favorites I never get tired of. Erin Brockovich was a regular person trying to make ends meet. She found a cause that moved her and was mainly interested in uncovering it. The financial abundance ended up coming in, even though that was not her concern when fighting for the underdog.

The Founder is another rags to riches film with Michael Keaton. It was based on the true story of Ray Kroc, the guy that created the McDonald's fast food chain. Opinions on him are across the board from people that loved him and those that loathed him. The point of this was that he was an unsuccessful salesperson, but somehow struck gold when he found something great in the McDonald's formula for fast food. He ended up rising up the ranks to major never-ending financial success.

Watching those rags to riches type films have left me feeling as if I was injected with newfound inspiration and optimism. Joyful experiences can help you get into a positive state, but so does aligning with God and Spirit. Putting your trust and faith into the universal heavenly forces above is better than any material abundance that can be offered.

A friend of mine went to a wedding with someone he was dating. He and his date found they were comparing themselves to the guests. They seemed better in both of their eyes by the status achieved. He explained that everyone at the wedding was accomplished and successful. They were also around the same age as he and his date. After the wedding, he and his date talked about it and felt like they were so far behind compared to the successful wedding patrons.

Comparing yourself to others can bring your vibrational energy down. Whether it's I'm better than you or you're better than me. Feeling like someone is better than you pulls you down harder because of the despair, disappointment, and frustration energy associated with it. You are not above or below me, because we are the same. Everyone has their own gifts and talents to offer to humanity for the greater good. Even if it's in the same genre you're interested in. Every single person has a distinctively unique way of offering those gifts and talents that will appeal to someone out there.

Working so hard and feeling as if you're getting nowhere fast can take its toll on you. You continue to struggle while others around you try something and hit instant success. You might find yourself getting critical, "I don't get it. They're younger than I am, have almost little to no work experience, or they're better looking than I am…."

This can easily cause a combination of depression and envy. There is no set time frame for achieving success. Everyone has their own timeline of when things will come about. For some, it may seem more instant, while another will struggle for much longer. It doesn't mean you're less than or not talented enough. Sometimes it's the more talented and gifted that take the longer way around to see the abundance flowing into their life effortlessly. They're gaining more knowledge and experience that others don't have through that longer process. It's like the Tortoise and the Hare story. The Tortoise moved slower, but ended up surpassing the Hare in the end in that fairy tale.

It's been known at this point that I started my work life in the film business when I was twenty-three years old working for a movie star actress at her company. All good blessings came down from that point where it opened more doors and job offers. I still receive notes from upcoming generations in their teens and young adulthood reaching out to me to ask how I got into the film business. Because the role I was brought in is not only difficult, but especially rare for the age I was at the time. They're trying to get in as well too.

I did reveal the cliff note version of that trajectory in the book I mentioned earlier, *"Reaching for the Warrior Within"*.

This isn't to rattle off a book plug. It's mentioned for those interested in that particular storyline trajectory that it's in that one. Basically, it took me seven years to get into the film business. I knew I would get in when I was sixteen, but it wasn't until I turned twenty-three when I finally got that lucky phone call out of the blue that changed my life. That was one of many major turning points and crossroads in my life. Getting in was persistence, passion, and dedication, but it was also a stroke of Divine luck. It was one call that changed my life and cracked open the abundant door. I always say getting in was luck, but staying in was talent. That goes for anything anyone does.

Stay strong, remain faithful, and full of hope, as you forge ahead undeterred by anything the darkness of ego throws at you. Everyone is moving at their own pace. Feeling frustration over the lack of results can make you want to give up and throw in the towel, but keep going and stay focused on your purpose and mission. Avoid comparing your trajectory to someone else's. You are needed, so please don't give up, but keep at it. You'll get there if it kills you. Your drive is your winning card, so don't allow someone else's success to squash what you are working on. Instead allow that to help you feel inspired and motivated to work even harder.

SELF-ESTEEM and SELF-LOVE

I've heard most everyone tell me that they can't stand the sound of their own voice, even though their voice is perfectly beautiful. A video or audio recording of them will be played back as they look in horror, "Is that how I sound? Turn that off!"

It's also why movie stars and actors have admitted it's difficult for them to watch themselves on screen. The one profession where someone has accepted their voice proudly are the singers and speakers of all types. They've learned to focus on their voice to such a high degree that they are accustomed to how it sounds. Their voice is the money, the gift, and their career.

Talking with this body builder at the gym, the conversation moved into vanity. He commented that I seemed exceptionally fit, although I disagreed explaining that I like taking care of myself, but I don't personally see it. I then added that he was. He said, "Oh no, I don't see it in myself either. I think I have that body dysmorphia something or rather."

That kicked off a discussion into how people view themselves differently than the way others do. I was surprised to find that even though to others he appeared built, muscular, and physically fit, that he didn't see that at all. His personal view of himself is skewed to an unrealistic level. This was one person out of thousands I've conversed with over what they perceive to be flaws in themselves.

In the past, I've discussed the process of external upkeep. Some body builders are extremely muscular to the point that others have explained it can be too much. They don't see themselves that way, so they continue pumping more iron than necessary that it becomes an unhealthy obsession. This has also been seen with some that partake in plastic surgery. Constantly having plastic surgery to the degree they become unrecognizable. They go beyond more than it was originally needed.

How about those people that have spent enormous amounts of money to look like a celebrity. They've paid anywhere from $20,000 to a $100,000 to change their appearance to match a famous person. You have to wonder where someone's mind is at on the self-esteem scale when you drop that kind of money for something that superficial, while kids are living in some kind of abusive impoverished situation with no funds to help. It falls in line with other toxic addictions. There is a lack of self-love for who you are. This is different than the basic aesthetic grooming beauty upkeep one enjoys like facials, skin-care, hair-care, physical work-out training, etc.

There are what could be considered genuine flaws to work on, such as if you're someone that has rage anger issues. Calling it a flaw may be the wrong word to describe it, and using the word challenge could be more appropriate. This particular kind of flaw or challenge is one you could admit, "I have anger issues. I'm aware of it and I have been working on trying to control it more."

That's a different kind of challenge that can be worked on to improve. What you might perceive to be a flaw in your appearance and looks is subjective. Learn to love everything about you. You change the things you're able to change, and you love and accept the areas that absolutely can never be improved.

Humanity is gravely obsessive over their physical appearance because the ego in humankind harshly judges one another by what they look like. The perception of who is considered beautiful or good looking would be vastly different if people saw one another's soul instead of the physical vessel they temporarily inhabit. Relationships would last longer because people would be merging together based on soul attraction rather than physical attraction, even though I understand that physical attraction helps at first, but that's only the start of coming together. Physical attraction fades no matter how good looking someone is. When you're younger you base the quality of a potential love partner solely on their physical attractiveness to you. As you grow older and more mature, the quality of a potential love partner is based on personality chemistry and the companionship factor

There would be less of an obsession to try and garner false attention through perfecting your exterior and more work done on your interior. Raising your consciousness and awareness level can help in rising above the superficial and diving beneath the surface to get to the root of who someone truly is. It can help you dive into getting to know who you really are too.

People that are hyper obsessed with their bodies, selfies, attention, and constant physical exterior adoration aren't fans of that kind of talk. They take it as an attack, even though the message is a generality to smarten up and dive beneath the superficiality. One needs a healthy dose of spiritual saving if they're more consumed with vanity than depth.

This isn't saying not to do your best to take care of yourself and look good in the areas you are able to, nor is it saying that there is anything wrong with finding yourself or someone physically attractive. It's about the borderline obsessiveness of being consumed wholly by your looks and basing your existence on whether or not your body is worshipped by others. External validation is a shallow goal.

I'm just as guilty since I've done the muscle flexing selfies, although I was never doing it as much as others. I've had people ask me to check out their Instagram. I head over there and notice their entire Instagram is nothing but hundreds of every selfie of them that you can imagine scrolling all the way down. It's concerning to see how deep they've fallen into the obsession of superficiality, attention, and adoration. They use their body and looks to gain false attention. What might be even more disconcerting is they get that attention. Thousands of people are liking and splattering it with attention, but it's shallow attention.

You might be wondering what does any of this have to do with abundance. Self-love and gratitude are magical elements to incorporate into your life that help in pushing that abundance door wide open. Anything and everything mentioned in this is connected to getting the flow of positive abundance moving. Everything I, and my Spirit team, discusses applies to myself as well. I'm also a constant work in progress and continuing to be as mindful and aware as possible. I'm always looking at the areas I can improve on.

This positive thinking isn't news when it comes to attracting in abundance. This is to continue to hammer home the feel good feelings to reach into ones psyche where you can feel inspired or more inspired than you are now. This is to feel content, good, and optimistic about where you are currently at and what's to come. It is to praise how hard you've come and how hard you've worked. Give yourself the credit for what you've accomplished to date.

Rapper Snoop Dogg received his star on the Hollywood Walk of Fame in 2018. I fell in love with his speech because he praises himself and gives himself the credit: *"Last but not least, I want to thank me for believing in me. I want to thank me for doing all this hard work. I want to thank me for having no days off. I want to thank me for never quitting. I want to thank me for always being a giver and trying to give more than I receive. I want to thank me for trying to do more right than wrong. I want to thank me for just being me at all times."*

This is amazing and brilliant. Some immediately get turned off or offended when anyone believes in themselves or props themselves up. They'll naively throw the ego or narcissistic word around with abandon. There is nothing wrong with applauding and giving yourself credit for the hard work you put in. You're the one doing the work, give yourself a round of applause! You can't rely on others to prop you up. Prop yourself up!

On one occasion, I was hanging with my former boss, the movie star actress, about three years into my employment with her. And I said, "You know I really have to thank you, because I could not have done all of these things I've done to date without your help and you opening that door."

She just point blank said, "Oh stop it, you did it yourself."

That forever stuck because I thought, "Actually you are right. I shouldn't be bowing down to others for the work I fought to do on my own."

External human validation isn't something I

require, because I know my worth through God. I know who I am, what I can do, and what I've done. Believe in yourself and give yourself credit when you do good things. Praising yourself is considered self-love that lifts your vibration up into the vortex of attracting in more good stuff.

CHAPTER ELEVEN

Improving Your Mind, Body, and Spirit

God, Spirit, and the Divine's energy moves through me. I, and you, are one with God. From as far back as ten years old, I could feel His energy pushing me forward to take care of myself on all levels from the mind, body, and soul spirit. From as seemingly minor as going for a jog or a bike ride to delving my mind into study and learning. Since my childhood years, fitness and exercise have forever been a big part of my life's interests without ever fading.

I can remember teaching myself to learn to ride a bike the same way I'd teach myself to do anything and everything I was interested in. We couldn't afford much growing up, so when the neighbor's were going out of town, one of my childhood friends allowed me to practice using his bike. It was diving into the practice, which helped me to teach myself to ride a bike. There was no one walking me through the steps. The Internet and You Tube instructional videos didn't exist in those days. I grabbed the bike and practiced on my own. I fell off it a number of times, but I picked myself up, picked the bike up, and continued on with the persistent practice until by the time the neighbor's came back I was an excellent bike rider. This is how I trained myself to do anything and everything I had a desire to learn. It was through the avenue of tough no-nonsense streets smarts and practice that would carry with me throughout my Earthly life.

I learned things through the school of hard knocks. This was by jumping on in and doing the work without any formal training. Due to my inhibiting ADD/ADHD, learning anything was fraught with some kind of disability anyway. I couldn't learn by sitting in a class listening to a lecture. I had to dive in and actually do the work.

Since I was a teenager, the major jobs I received throughout my life consisted of me being the one candidate with zero experience for the job being interviewed for. In the end, I was the candidate they went with. I was able to convince them I could excel at whatever it was they gave me. I might be rusty at first, but give me a few trial runs and they will be unable to find a harder worker that can master it over someone with the education and experience. It was this passion coupled with my forthright fighting nature that was my winning card.

This proved true as many of those employers later commented long after I left the employment that they chose well when taking that risk to go with the person without the credentials or experience only to be blown away. These employers who remained in contact with me long after I left all had informed me they were unable to find a suitable replacement that could do what I did for them.

This has been my mantra throughout my life. Be a fighter in all you do. Have passion, persistence, drive, and a strong will to do the job fast and fearless. I've always had an interest in being completely aware, conscious, and driven to be the best I can be. My interest and focus on expanding my mind, strengthening my body, and nourishing my soul were present since childhood. I've persistently been a huge promoter of taking care of yourself on all levels. This advocacy includes the body through fitness, exercise, and nutrition.

Even when I fell into my young adult party days of alcohol, drugs, and cigarettes in my early twenties, I was still conscious enough to work out hard if I was going to be putting those toxins in my body. I was drinking carrot and cucumber juices since I was seventeen, even during my party in a cup days.

Luckily, the partying days evaporated by the time I was moving into my mid-to-late twenties, My main focus moved right into fitness and exercise. I knew that a strong body was necessary. This had nothing to do with vanity, which is why some work out. There has been evidence that some people work out and take care of themselves more while single, but as soon as they end up in a long-term relationship they get lazy about it. My desire to exercise and work out regularly is partially because I always feel incredible afterwards. If I was feeling low or depressed, I would go for a run or endure a rigorous work out. Suddenly I was feeling stronger and more alive than I had ever been!

The stronger I grew through physical fitness, the stronger my Divine psychic connections became. It also helped me make it through the long days of juggling my day job work life to building my side business life purpose career.

I run into people today and many have commented, "You are so fit!" Never mind the positive side effect that it helps you look good, but what's more important is that I feel incredible! Today I run circles around others that are two to three times younger than I am. It's not me who notices this, but they have consistently pointed this out to me themselves.

This isn't about being better than anyone else, but about motivating others to do the same. Because you have to care about your body the way you care about other things you have interest in. How can one neglect that physical vessel you were temporarily gifted with?

I know there will be a day when I may physically not be able to do certain things. Although, one friend once informed me that he and another friend of ours was in Joshua Tree National Park on a particular occasion. As it was getting dark, they noticed a female figure racing down the rocks from up high. She was incredibly fit racing towards them until she slowed down in front of them. He said she might have been in her sixties when they first noticed her. They talked to her and were surprised to learn that she was in her nineties! She's been doing that exercise for decades and feels great.

My mouth was on the floor, "Wow, that's incredible! I love hearing stories like that. I want to be like that if I'm still around in my nineties."

I received a huge rush of joy and excitement to know that it could be possible.

God gave you this temporary body to house your soul so that you may live an Earthly physical human life full of lessons, experiences, blessings, and challenges. You have to take care of all parts of you body, mind, and soul. All three of these are what the spiritual genre was comprised of, but that's mainly because these are the important aspects that make up the totality of you.

Some people avoid exercise or express disdain and reach for those potato chips and ice cream day after day, feeling even more lethargic than the day before. Many shun study and higher learning while instead trying to find their next conquest to have sex with. Maybe this means nothing to you, but you would be surprised by the amount of messages I receive from people regularly that send me inappropriate messages, as if I'm just a body to use. One would think you should be flattered. When you have an expanded mind, but the intelligence is uninteresting to someone, then that comes off more offensive to me.

I'm highly aware of what people are interested in because I receive this from them every single week. They only have one thing on their mind. Attempting to have any kind of intellectual deep conversation is met with resistance through their one to two word answers of disinterest in talking about anything beyond physical pleasure. It's about how quickly can you come here and give it to me, for lack of a better phrase. I've had some friends say, "I feel like you need to dumb it down with some of the others."

It's never been said as an attack or harsh judgment, but as sage advice. They know having a raised consciousness and higher intelligence level in an Earthly world dominated and ruled by the darkness of ego, the superficial, and shallow, that it can be a lonely place for that soul. This has been a common theme complaint from the spiritually based crowd. Many of them have been raising their consciousness and intelligence through knowledge gaining, study, and experiences. They've found it difficult to relate or connect to others that weren't interested in any of that.

The more superficial you are, then the more popular you become. The masses love superficiality, shallowness, and a hyper focus on the exterior. They want to see hard young bodies, fancy cars and mansions. It doesn't matter what that person has to say as long as they fit that description. In fact, the social media user only needs to post that without any caption and it will garner hundreds of thousands and millions of people giving the thumbs up and applause. This isn't a criticism or judgment, but the current sad reality. The evidence is in plain sight for all to see.

Many shun deepening their soul and consciousness through spiritual and religious studies coupled with hard driven life experiences. What good is life if the three components of body, mind, and soul that make up basic healthy survival are ignored and discarded.

Work on making healthier life choices. This includes your diet and drink intake as well as adequate regular exercise, pending you are physically able to. You might be someone that is physically unable to exercise due to human physical challenges this lifetime. This is not directed to those that cannot physically do it due to a handicap or physical issue. This is directed to those who are capable of physical exercise, but don't want to out of laziness or because they hate it.

When you take care of yourself on all levels, then this has an effect on your overall well-being. Having a strong well-being has a positive effect on your mood and thoughts. This simultaneously elevates the vibration of both your feelings and thoughts, which makes you a powerful abundance attractor. Joy brings in more joy and sadness brings in more sadness. Which would you like to have?

This isn't saying you're not allowed to have any fun. Having fun is an essential luxury. When you operate in high octane stress mode attending to daily practical matters, then you risk burn out.

You also raise your stress levels, which drops your vibration. A low vibration can diminish the potential of attracting in positive abundance. Perhaps you don't care for the theory that pushes you to be positive and avoid negativity. How many people do you know that are perpetually negative, but are simultaneously attracting in all sorts of positive abundance. I don't know of many cases where that exists. I've heard of more cases where someone is a positive optimistic go-getter and is simultaneously attracting in awesome great things in their life.

Get up off the couch and out of a dull mindset and get to work. Create a sanctuary in a private space in your house where you can connect to God and receive profound insights, messages, and guidance that urge you to make positive changes in your life. Pay attention to these messages and take action on them.

If your Spirit team is urging you to get outside and exercise, then follow that advice. They know that when you take care of your body that you become a ferocious Divine communicator that helps you make powerfully positive choices that bring your goals and dreams to fruition. Suddenly the flow of positive abundance starts to move in your direction. Fitness and exercise breathes new life into your soul. It helps dissolve or reduce any negative emotions such as depression or stress. You feel an uplifting crystal clear calm focus that enables you to put action into your goals that makes great things happen.

Don't beat yourself up if you find exercise

difficult at first. The more you do it the easier it gets, where it eventually becomes like oxygen to you. If two days have passed and I have not exercised, I can feel it. I can feel it in my body and entire state of being. I can feel it in my psychic senses pushing me to soar forward freely in an exercise routine. I have to dive on in before I go crazy. I'm then transported into the soul of the Divine with this essence moving throughout my entire body. Great ideas soon rise to the forefront over what I need to do and accomplish.

Whenever I have an unresolved problem, I go directly to God the ultimate source of guidance. I don't rely on human beings to prop me up and change my life. I rely on God to help prop me up and change my life. He has that power having proven it to me time and again.

It's no one else's job to cheer you up, bring you joy, or lavish you with attention. Stop expecting other people to take on the responsibility of bringing you joy. Stop being dependent on others to prop you up, fix you, and give you devotion. And stop getting angry when others are not catering to you the way you want them to. Doing that will only result in frustration and bitterness, which is the perfect breeding ground for the Darkness to grow. No one can fulfill that impossible demand, Anyone with any measure of a healthy self-esteem won't stick around and bow down to that kind of energy.

It is your responsibility to create your own joy and prop yourself up. Avoid relying on people to remind you of your worth. Pull yourself up by your bootstraps, stand tall, and know your worth by empowering yourself through Source. When you've excelled at reaching that space where you no longer need or require any of that from others, then does all the good stuff start to fall into place naturally on its own. And even if it doesn't, you could careless as you're not craving validation anyway.

This joy seeking attention from others is more about the co-dependent and toxic like relationships that others rely on. It is not necessarily about the healthier balanced relationships where you feel joy being around your partner as they do with you. There may be some that fall into the space of needing constant attention from others, whether it's from a lover, friends, family members, or strangers. They love messages of joy, but fail to notice when they have been guilty of falling into the co-dependency aspect part of it.

Today many find it hard to believe that I was once a co-dependent person while in my early twenties. I mistakenly put too much dependence on other people to prop me up and fix me. Luckily, it was only a matter of years in where I realized that it wasn't working. People cannot fulfill that kind of unrealistic demand from another person. One of the top keywords friends have repeatedly used in describing me with others is, "He's very independent."

It's pretty common to seek out attention and love from external sources from the teenage years on up into ones early twenties. One hopes that by the time you begin moving into your later twenties, your desire for external sources to shower you with love fades. You realize that it can be conjured up naturally by standing in your own power.

Exercise does a body good on all levels for this reason. It helps in raising your vibration, energy, and consciousness where you feel alive without the validation of others. You look and feel incredible. It cracks open the psychic line with the other side even more. It also helps you heal from illnesses that are healable much quicker.

Without wanting to jinx it, I haven't had the full blown flu in fifteen years at the point of this book. Some have asked me what's my secret? The last time I was bed ridden with a dramatic flu was fifteen years ago. And technically, when I was getting sick in those days, it was usually from catching it from someone else that was around me. I eventually grew to be so strict that I refused to be around anyone that had a cold or the flu until they were better. It doesn't mean I'm unkind, because if they are someone close to me, I am buying all sorts of healing remedies and a goodie bag that I leave at their door.

This doesn't mean I don't get sick or haven't been sick since, but I just haven't been bed ridden for days or even a day for that matter. I have however felt the initial hints of a potential flu coming onto me. I'm highly aware when something with my body has suddenly shifted. I might have crossed paths with someone that was sick, so I start to feel a bit weak. The second I suspect anything, I immediately always up my game and begin the process of the preventatives, the exercise, the higher intake of vitamin C supplements and foods, and more water than usual.

I also pray to God and call in the healing Archangel Raphael to help prevent what I'm feeling to blow up into more. I believe in both medicinal healing remedies coupled with spiritual healing remedies, then I follow all of this by going to bed earlier than usual. Nine times out of ten, I wake up the next morning energized and ready to seize the day. No signs of the illness anymore. It was completely knocked out of the park.

This goes back to being in tune to your body, mind, and soul. Be aware of everything happening around and within you every second. Notice all changes and shifts that take place within you. If it's a challenge coming upon you, then take care of it as fast as possible. Take care of you. Be disciplined about you, yourself, your body, mind and soul. Take it seriously and don't ignore the subtle hints and shifts within and around you. Those can be guidance or messages coming in from the Divine.

CHAPTER TWELVE

*Clearing the Chaos Within and Around
Your Soul and Surroundings*

Another step for preparing you to open the floodgates of abundance may cause some fuss. This is cleaning and clearing the clutter in your life, both internally and externally. It can be clearing out friendships that only bring you down and make you feel bad about yourself, to cleaning up and organizing your home life. Messy discombobulated surroundings can create a disrupted flow of positive abundance.

You can really get into it by consulting with a Feng Shui expert. If this is too costly or doesn't interest you, then do some free research online to gain some basic tips. The clearing of the clutter doesn't need to be perfect, but you might feel you can get more organized than you might be right now. If you walk into your home and you see the disarray with items piled sky high, then take one section at a time to get your home organized. Disorganization disrupts the energy flow in and around your life.

Be mindful of the kind of people you hang around with as they can affect your aura and energetic field as well too. If you're around someone who is a perpetual toxic person, then you will absorb that into your being and will become one with it. Work on dissolving connections that offer you no positive benefit. You don't have to abruptly cut people out, but if you are looking to reduce your contact with them, or dissolve them out of your life, then work on dissolving people the way you dissolve any toxic vice, which is gradually, safely, and slowly. You are available for them less and less over time.

This isn't about abandoning people in a time of need. This is about the offenders that only use you to harshly rant and complain about something regularly that they have no interest in improving. You make constructive suggestions to help them, which is met with retaliation and resistance. Follow this by keeping your options open to add in new friendships with those you feel a stronger connection with that are enjoyable to be around and more aligned with who you are or are becoming.

The other benefits to clearing the clutter within and around you is that it contributes to helping you think more clearly. The flow of energy moves swiftly than if you were living in chaotic disarray. When the energy is moving positively, this brings in positivity. When you live in chaos, then that's what you invite in. After my father passed away, I was stunned to discover how he had been living in such disorder. Nonsense piled sky high covering every inch of space that could be found filled with something.

Sometimes the clutter can come up in the least likely of places. One of the positives of the Internet is that you can purchase most anything you desire without so much as a thought. You can do that from anywhere, such as from your phone in bed in the middle of the night when you can't sleep. You no longer have to fight the traffic and crowds to get a good parking spot at a store, then spend all of that time browsing the aisles, and standing in line to purchase those items.

It's so rare and infrequent that I physically walk into a store. The majority of everything is delivered to me, including groceries! This isn't out of laziness, since others have explained I'm one of the least laziest people they know. Part of the delivery bit is the convenience, but the other part of it is due to my severe social anxiety and the tampering of chaotic psychic energies absorbed while going to a crowded place filled with disgruntled people like in a retail store.

The downfall to this case of ordering stuff online is that there are now numerous statistics popping up all over the place indicating a dreadful vision. The world in general is hoarding more products they don't need due to impulsive online shopping. There was a point I had walked into my place and noticed all of these items sitting around in boxes that were delivered. My heart sunk in a feeling of devastation. I couldn't believe what I had allowed to happen, "What is all this? How do I have all this stuff? For what purpose?"

I decided to give it away to people who could use it. Giving away clothes sent to me by that label that I never wore or took the tags off. Labels and vendors send me stuff on top of that due to the position I'm in. I had become what I thought I would never be….a hoarder. Luckily, it wasn't a lifetime of collecting, but more like several weeks. This was several weeks too long that I had to get rid of it all. If I've never used it, then I never will. I then looked up local charities and places where people were suffering from material lack and brought it to them.

Most people have admitted the stuff they buy they don't really need. They end up throwing it away creating a bigger trash situation. This is a planet of hoarding! It's become another addiction even for those who don't like shopping. They hit, "add to cart", and then click that "buy" button and a rush of Dopamine lifts them up.

Dopamine is that high happy feeling one gets from things like food, drugs, alcohol, sex, shopping, and on and on. It is anything that makes someone feel good….temporarily. Because once that high drops astronomically, which it will sooner than later, you crash suddenly feeling low again and out in search of another fix. You race to get that addictive fix like a drug injection that gives you another temporary high to keep going.

Some consume this false happiness where they do this daily just to stay happy and keep going. It never lasts and winds up leaving you craving another fix again. When the package you ordered arrives, that dopamine fix hits you again to open that brand new package. But what do you do with that package after opening it? Some never even take it out of the wrapper. It gets tossed aside to sit on the counter for a week or two until you mumble, "I need to put this away. I never even took this out of the wrapper."

Because of the ease of buying online, you're not paying much attention to how often you add to your cart and click purchase. There are people who are exceptional at watching what they spend. Some don't have the money, or they don't own a credit card, and they're just trying to get by with the basics. For others, myself included, I've had to learn to be extra cautious. I'm usually cautious as it is, but sometimes I'm looking at what's being delivered and wondering, "Did I really need this contraption? What possessed me to buy this?"

It took some additional self-discipline to realize I was being sucked into the new trend of online shopping and hoarding without realizing it. Compared to others it wasn't as bad as I'm not that much of an impulsive shopper. I've never liked shopping unless there was something specific I needed. I wasn't one of those people buying additional pairs of shoes or clothes I knew I would never wear.

I'm the opposite extreme where I've worn the same pairs of shoes until they grow torn. That's my cue to buckle down and get a better pair of shoes. I never bought the latest iPhone, but would use the same version for years long past its upgrade eligibility date. I'd keep using it until key features like the home button would stop working. That would be clue that it was time to buckle down and change the phone because the buttons are no longer working.

While some people revel in the latest gadget craze, I saw no difference. Plus the hassle to transferring everything over to the new device was too much of a chore that was never worth it to me. If the phone still works, then I'm keeping it.

Other things to keep in mind are that manufacturers are using cheaper materials to make items, which means they break or tear sooner than later, so you have to keep buying the same gadget or item repeatedly over the years. I had regular oscillator fans that seemed less powerful in its breeze a year after it was bought. I soon realized I had to keep replacing them the way you change your tires or brakes regularly on your car.

Clothes are also getting holes or shrinking sooner than later after a few washes. You have to replace those regularly. While the trend to be more environmentally safe or conscious has risen, that hasn't necessarily shown when it comes to how much material is being dumped into landfills. According to many statistics, that number has increased astronomically, which means the environmental craze hasn't improved much.

Many Universities and Colleges have reported enormous shocking statistics surrounding how much waste students collect or are unused. Tons of waste is discarded or donated if the student hasn't bothered to do it after vacating their dorms. The waste that the planet tosses on a large basis can make anyone with a heart, soul, or conscious break down. It's an eye opener when you know about this massive waste and that there are people around the world struggling to survive barely able to afford food. The amount of waste that could be donated to organizations that can help people in need is staggering. There is no mobilization, protest, or marching over circumstances like poverty or child abuse.

A great deal of stuff donated to places like the Goodwill aren't getting sold there either. They end up getting dumped in a landfill as well in the end. You order something online because it's easy. You think it's no big deal if the item isn't what you wanted in the end, because you can return it. When it comes to returning items bought online, a great deal of people have admitted they don't bother, because it takes a bit more effort to find packaging for it, printing out the proper return slips and receipt, then driving down to the mail carrier service. Most people find it's not worth it to go through all that unless it was a super expensive item.

How does this all tie into abundance attracting? A messy house, aura, ambiance, surroundings, and life contributes to messy abundance attraction energy. It creates a block due to the restricted flow of your physical surroundings. If you are a sensitive in tune being, then you no doubt have noticed that when you've walked into a cluttered filled room that you can feel the dark weight of that. When you walk into a space that is free of clutter, then this uplifting feeling rises inside you. Everything in and around you has an effect on your well-being state, including the things you would never consider to have an effect.

Conduct regular space clearing exercises where throughout each year you periodically walk around your house and examine what needs to be boxed up and put away. Look at what needs to be re-organized and set up in a better way. Move furniture around if you have to in order to create a more ideal set up, which can assist in the flow of abundance energy.

When you walk through each room of your house, how do you feel? Are you disappointed at the mess? Do you feel joyful and clear minded? Do you feel a heaviness?

Any negative feeling felt is a clue that some re-organizing needs to be conducted. If you find you're too busy or you keep putting it off, then set a disciplined schedule. This can be where you rely on the seasons changing to re-organize. When it's the first week of Spring, Summer, Fall, and Winter. Use those dates to begin the space clearing if you're someone that procrastinates or keeps putting it off. Light some sage and candles to help purify the air, open your windows daily if for at least fifteen minutes to an hour to clear the old air with the new one. I know that can be tougher to do in colder climates, but do what you can and when you can. You know what you can tolerate and get away with without it harming your comfort or health.

When you sage your home, pay attention to corners of your house where energy gets stuck. As someone with Clairvoyance, I've seen darkness in corners of homes and buildings, which show up as floods of insects. There is trapped dark energy in corners more than in any other spot. Have the intention of ridding it as you Sage and clear your space. Also pay attention to doorways, which can be entryways for toxic dark spirits.

Clear your aura and spirit, which you can do with Sage smoke around your body as well too. You can take a cleansing shower or bath with Epsom salts and essential oils, or you can simply have the intention of clearing your aura by calling in Archangel Michael, Archangel Raphael, or Archangel Jophiel to clear you and your space of any toxic negative energy in all directions of time.

Part of cleansing you, your space and home with Sage, is also paying especially important care to your bed area. You most likely spend a great deal of time in bed. It's important to clear that energy regularly. If you go to bed in any negative state or if the night is met with tossing and turning, negative feelings, thoughts, or bad dreams, then ensure you clear the bed with Sage or whatever tools you prefer to purify it as a precaution.

Sometimes all you need to do is sit or stand in silence and prayer, eyes closed, and mentally call in

God, your Spirit team, and only those beings of the highest vibrational nature. You can say something like, *"Please clear me now of all negative toxic energy I've absorbed or created in all directions of time. And so it is."*

You might choose to create an alter, or sacred space, in your home used primarily for prayer or to help you get more spiritually focus. Burn candles and diffuse nice smells with essential oils to incense, sage, or cedar burning. Candles are great to help give you a focal point. The light of a candle is also welcoming for angels who enjoy the light that is not harsh or tampered with such as artificial or florescent light.

Be careful with your tech gadgets and how they're situated near your bed. There are also growing scientific statistics showing the negative effects on you and your well-being when tech gadgets are so close to you while sleeping. It's more likely than not most people tend to have their cell phones near them all the time. They've become extensions of us. Imagine what that's like and the repercussions that can come out of that. A great many people also live in smaller places or apartments where it's not realistic to hide where their computer equipment is situated. You do the best you can with how you're setting it up, so that it's not affecting your well-being and sleep.

CHAPTER THIRTEEN

The Power of Nature

*I*mproving your psychic senses simultaneously improves your spiritual connection with the Divine. Some find anything connected to psychic phenomena as being of the Devil, but the irony is having a strong connection with God comes through your psychic senses. Others will strongly disagree with something and call it evil without having any knowledge of it enough to be making a comment. That's been going on since the dawn of humanity.

They may be confusing the possibility that having a strong psychic antennae can invite in negative spirits. Negative spirits will attack whoever they can get close to, including a non-believer, a believer, or someone psychically in tune, so that theory is null and void. There are also numerous cases of a dark spirit attaching itself to a devout religious follower, so the belief that a dark spirit can only be conjured up by a Medium also isn't bathed in truth.

Strengthening your psychic clair senses helps with increasing your faith and being able to follow the guidance coming in from above. Many of the guidance that's been suggested throughout this book have touched on the different ways to improve and strengthen your psychic antennae. Not only do these guidance suggestions help to perfect your well-being, but that simultaneously improves your psychic radar, all of which assist in opening up the floodgates of abundance.

Getting out into a nature setting can assist the soul in reaching that level of awakening. It is far easier for Spirit to access someone when they're in a calming environment such as a nature setting. Many purport to feeling much calmer after taking a stroll in nature. I'm a fan of all things connected to nature, which includes the deserts and badlands with its dry terrain and extensive geological erosions that cast into a breathtaking color display of volcanic rock, canyons, and mesas. Those areas have always proven great escapes to commune with my higher council through the winds as the sage Native American Wise Ones once did in massive numbers across North America. All that remains are the clues left behind in entombed sediments of extinct fossils of tribal skulls and dinosaur-like creatures that no longer roam the Earth, but whose presence is profoundly felt.

Spirit communication travels along the particles of oxygen, so where there is wind there is spirit in grave numbers. It gives you an opportunity for reflection, redemption, and answers. Just like Bob Dylan said in his song, *"The answer my friend is blowing in the wind."*

The Divine answers are travelling along with the wind. The sense of time while in those nature places is what hits you. You realize we have a short shelf lifespan. You hear that from others of older age that it flies by, so you better take advantage of the time you have while here. As a teenager at a party, I was conversing with this woman in her thirties. I still remember her saying, "Make your choices today. I wish I knew then what I know now."

What she said forever stuck for me because I knew what she was talking about. I knew that a human life goes by superfast, so don't waste one minute not getting into your work and diving into your purpose. Otherwise you'll wake up one day and look in the mirror and wonder where the time went. I remember being in panicked mode around age fifteen and sixteen realizing that I need to get moving and get to work as my life is flying by. This was as a teenager. I was hyper aware of what was up ahead while here. I've talked to people that reach older age when it truly hits them. They were young and vibrant with the whole world at their feet. After years of disappointments, what they once dreamed of seemed to grow impossible and unlikely to transpire. They may look their age, but inside feel as if they're still sixteen. Continue to expand your mind and consciousness beyond the routine.

There are various reasons I love all nature power places. It offers quiet contemplation through Divine spirit connecting. It also gives you an injection of reality along with a wider perspective that can easily get lost when you fall into the superficiality or the mundane of physical life.

When I was twenty years old, I knew those shallow interests were great for five minutes, but I needed more than that. I needed to be challenged. I was a sponge screaming inside for more than what people gave me through Earthly patterns. There was no way I could endure living with a mediocre mindset, even if that meant I would be set apart from everyone else, which I was regardless.

In vast nature settings, your view broadens and opens up. You see who you are in comparison to this temporary home of a planet. Things like social media suddenly seem trivial in contrast. All of the wrangling on it does nothing to attract any kind of a positive abundant mindset, but instead dulls the spirit senses, your life force, and vibrational energy unless you are using it for good and positivity. Living hypnotized by the toxic allure and superficial triviality gossip every second can be depressing. Some believe it's natural to remain in a superficial state, because it's what's taught. While some of it can be fun once in awhile, to endure that indefinitely can be miserably medieval.

Have faith and believe what you desire will

come. Believe you are deserving of good. Be open and receptive to receive. Ensure you're balancing giving and receiving. This is by not overdoing one without the other. This imbalance can block the positive movement flow. Examine what it is your desires are and what work you're willing to put in to achieve your goals.

Take action and be persistent with it. Helping the movement along positively means putting in the work. Kicking back dreaming of desires to come to fruition doesn't help those desires come to life. Dreaming of desires is a great step to take. It's the dreams in your mind and visions that start out like a seed. These dreams gradually begin to develop in your mind for awhile, much like a human pregnancy until that moment when you give birth to your dreams, as if you're giving birth to a child. Once that happens, you initiate action steps that can help the dreams grow and evolve.

Have a plan and know what you want, so as not to confuse the positive attraction quotient. Take regular time outs, retreats, and vacations. This helps alleviate stress, opens your psychic clair senses, and brings great ideas in. It helps elevate your vibration since people tend to be in a brighter spirits when they take a break. Study, perfect, and expand your mind and consciousness. All of this helps in cracking open the door to abundance.

Let's move to the final section in the next chapters of our abundance curriculum. Now that you've gained Divinely guided tips to improve and evolve your soul. Let's push open the Divine gates to abundance.

PART 3

»»� decorative border«««

Opening the Floodgates to Abundance

»»✦incomplete decorative border«««

CHAPTER FOURTEEN

Abundance Blocks –
Part One

A wide variety of abundance blocks are the culprit behind preventing the positive flow of profusion from streaming into someone's life. Up ahead in the remaining chapters are some suggestions as to what some of those general abundance blocks in your life can be. These are generalities since it's unlikely you will be living the exact same life as another person. Each case would need to be examined as to what could be blocking the positive flow of abundance in your life compared to another person's.

There are many factors to include when dissecting the ultimate make-up of each person's life circumstances, personality traits, and upbringing on the planet. There are also numerous reasons and steps to consider when it comes to identifying what your own abundance blocks are. Allow some of what is brought up here to resonate. If needed you can come back to this to write certain things down if it helps. This way you can hone in on some of what you believe could be an abundant block in your life. My team and I can point you in the general direction, but it is up to you to conduct this exercise with your own team of guides and angels. The reason is everyone's life trajectory is dissimilar from another person's.

Some of what's discussed may or may not trigger up particular memories you're transported back to. These are recollections of past memories where you know for certain the circumstance most definitely created an abundance block in your life.

An even further far-fetched notion is that blocks could have been created for your soul in lives before this one. You're unaware that your soul is still experiencing similar patterns from previous lives. This can make these upcoming chapters all the more worth while because it can help bring up stuff for you to review and evaluate. This review process helps you to bring it up and then banish it completely, so you can stop the cycle from repeating.

It's like someone who was repeatedly abused by a parent. That parent was abused by their parent and on and on backwards into time. The cycle ends when you or the abused person chooses not to follow in their parents footsteps. I know I came from this kind of a background from an abusive parent who was abused by their parent in some way on and on backwards. I chose to stop that cycle with me. With the assistance of your own Spirit team, you may start to become aware of what some of these blocks are while reading.

Consider all potential possibilities as to what the abundance blocks are. These are ones that can be attributed and created by your overall personality nature to your upbringing. What is your overall personality nature like? Are you typically an optimist or a pessimist? Are you a go-getter or do you wait for someone to do things for you? Are you practical and rational, or feeling oriented when it comes to general decisions made? What was your upbringing like? Were things handed to you or did you have to work hard for it? When things are handed to a child, then the child grows up expecting it. Whereas if a child never received anything and was always pushed down, that child has the ability to grow stronger and more resilient.

Who were the primary influencers during childhood that had an impact on who you are today? This is not who you admire that had a positive impact on you, even though those personalities certainly help shape you as well too. This is about who was around you and your state of being growing up, whether or not you had a good relationship with them or not. This would include your caregivers, parents, or guardians. It would also include family members, friendships, teachers, and fellow students. All of that plays a part into what may have created particular abundance blocks.

When an abundance block is formed early on in life, it doesn't fade away as you grow older. It is still part of your soul's DNA and imprint. It can have a positive or negative energy effect depending on how life goes for you or not.

Add to your list the positive elements in your life that helped in reducing some of these abundance blocks. This can be someone good around you that offered positivity to your world. Sometimes that's a teacher, a best friend, or even a popular singer that preaches about going after your dreams, which helped to inspire you early on. It's predominately in childhood and teenage years when one tends to look up to popular entertainers for motivation and inspiration. You might have had your favorite popular entertainer whose pictures you had plastered all over your bedroom wall growing up.

A popular entertainer may not always be the best influence, but as a teenager our perception is slightly skewed and rose colored due to being impressionable. You're transitioning from childhood to adulthood, which has some of the greatest impact on who you will become. This can have a positive or negative influence depending on who you were idolizing. It remains with you throughout adulthood even if you're no longer a fan of that particular artist. A mentor, teacher, fellow student, or friend could also have positively influenced you. It can go both ways where you are being influenced positively and negatively early on depending on whom you were surrounded by.

As you move into your twenties, you continue to be easily influenced by those around you. Generally by the time one crosses the Saturn Return transition between ages 28-30 primarily do you become set in your ways. You become less influenced in such a profound way that you might have been before that time period. You are not as influenced with such depth by much as you move past aged thirty. Even though you may admire other teachers, they don't have as much of an effect on your developmental process. All of this can have positive or detrimental effects to how effortless or not the abundance flows freely into your life. You can see at this point that there are abundance blocks formed without one realizing it.

Because finances and money are one of the greater obsessions when it comes to abundance, we're using finances and money as the example. This can still be lack of abundance in the love department with love and relationships. You would also look at the similar aspects discussed when it comes to find out what is blocking you from love.

What is your relationship with money like in general? Has it been easy to come by? Does it keep slipping through your fingers? Do you always seem to have just enough to survive comfortably, but never much more than that?

Money gives you the ability to physically survive, but it also has the added bonus of purchasing luxuries and goods. These are material items that you don't need to survive, but they're things that you want. You want that latest album by your favorite music artist, but it's not a life or death need to have it to physically survive. God looks at what you physically need for survival and not necessarily what you want and crave, although it's not a sin to buy that album for the fun and enjoyment of it. Music is one of the tools that can help raise your vibration.

Certain luxuries are beneficial to help raise your vibration and give you a positive state of well-being. It helps balance out your life, so that it's not always all work and no play. Play and luxury can be fed through music and those fun purchases that give you a bit of a lift. Balance work and play to ensure that you are vibrating at optimum levels. If your life is imbalanced, then this also plays a big part at creating an abundance block. Imbalanced life equates to imbalanced energy. If energy isn't balanced, then it cannot draw in balanced blessings.

Money is essentially energy, which means it can change form depending on how you think of or use it. It is what you do with it that can turn it into good or evil. There is no true separation between you and abundance. It may feel as if the vibrational discord between you and abundance is wide, but when you abolish the mentality of having a lack of abundance, then the closer that you and abundance move towards one another until you've merged successfully with it.

Abundance blocks are often embedded deeply in your subconscious that you may not even be aware of it being there Many abundance blocks go all the way back to your childhood and the main influencers in your life during the developmental childhood stages. Did you grow up in a household where people complained negatively about money? If the answer is yes, then this has seeped into your subconscious.

Someone else's complaint about money only needs to be made once in a big way for it to marinate into your aura and become a part of who you are. Look at your mother's view of money and what that was like. You can also use your guardian or the person you considered to be the mother figure in your life. What was the maternal energy about money around you like?

My own mother's view on money was she would repeatedly say the words, "I'm broke." Or, "I don't have any money."

She said those phrases so often it sounded like a broken hit record. It wasn't so much that she was living paycheck to paycheck, but even as a child those words were annoyingly negative in my consciousness. Those words rubbed me the wrong way to hear. I was extremely conscious of it while it was happening that it would get under my skin. Being consciously aware of the vibrational energy of those words made me despise that attitude anyone conveyed. That's pretty massive for an eight year old to be mindful of that early on. The result was that she forever struggled financially, never truly having much drive for anything nor striving for anything. She battled low self-esteem, was stressed, and struggled with money.

I've come across others that would say similar lines and would forever be stuck on pause of never having enough money. They ensured this would remain the case through their words. This isn't said with disdain or to look down on someone, but it's that I could see the detrimental effects it was having on their life early on. It pained me they couldn't see that either. Because I don't want to see anyone miserable the way the angels or God doesn't enjoy seeing that kind of misery in anyone. It's not in judgment, but more about that we can see the positivity that could happen in your life if you change your general attitude.

I understand what it's like to live check to check, work so hard, and feel as if nothing in the way of positive abundance is coming in. I understand because I've been there too. During those days, when I was living that kind of life, I could never consider or bring myself to say the low vibrational words of "I'm broke". Saying that phrase has an underlying feeling of, "Please feel sorry for me and give me money."

It's a heaviness that ends up pulling you down to the oceans floor by a depressing anchor. I was aware I needed to increase my income, but I never said, "I'm broke." I've said, "I need to budget right now."

That statement is more controlled and focused rather than, "I'm destitute." It's not denying or pretending you don't have money when you don't. It's just shifting your attitude about it. Because feeling miserable over anything won't increase your bank account or your feelings of well-being, so you may as well work to shift that to a less harmful word or phrase to describe your current financial situation.

Once you've looked at how your mother's view of money was growing up, then look at your father's view of money. What was that like? You can also use your guardian or the person that fulfilled the father role for you growing up. For some it can be one person that fulfilled the role of both parents. That still counts towards how you were influenced early on with finances. What were your father's issues with money?

My father was money hungry spending his life chasing finances. He made good money during the first part of his adult life, but was always trying to achieve more. He soon started to get money in deceitful ways where it ultimately created a bigger block by preventing a natural flow of money from coming in. It almost seemed as if he would try to get money out of anyone he would cross paths with.

He was a workaholic obsessed about making money and getting it from anyone he could, even if it meant through underhanded means. He was like an evil warden collecting everyone's money. I never felt that his work life was done for the passion of it, but merely to make money. Ultimately, he ended up in way over his head towards the end of his life when the finances coming in were less and less. This was partially due to his obsessional views of money. That kind of stress over money placed too much pressure on his heart and soul that he passed away months after his sixty-first birthday.

This is an example of just another block that is passed onto you without realizing it. Imagine the many other abundance blocks that have been generated because of the people you grew up with. This includes who you surrounded yourself with growing up and throughout the course of your life leading up to today. If you have friends that perpetually complain about being broke, then this seeps into your consciousness as well too. All it takes is one block to prevent the positive flow of abundance from coming in, even if the block is happening to someone else around you. If they are vocal about it with you, then it is penetrating into your aura.

Let's continue to look at some of the additional potential abundance blocks in the next chapter.

CHAPTER FIFTEEN

Abundance Blocks –
Part Two

Other abundance blocks can include feeling abandoned by God or abandoned by other people. If you feel rejected or abandoned, then that is considered energy you're sitting in according to God's law. This energy transfers to other areas of your life such as with abundance. You have the soul power to be a magical manifester. This means you have energy within and around you to direct it however you choose. If you choose not to be mindful of it, then it will spread recklessly in directions you wouldn't want it to go in.

If you subconsciously feel as if abundance has abandoned you, then work on changing that mindset. Work on a new belief system where you are deserving of abundance and know that it has not forsaken or deserted you.

Throughout my life, I've heard those of lesser means criticize rich people or see them as bad and evil. Feeling as if rich people are evil is a block as well too. The envious feelings block the flow of abundance. I have rich and poor friends, and they are some of the nicest giving people I know, so that criticism that rich people are evil isn't true with those I know. There are evil people in all economic brackets, just as there are evil people in all faiths and political beliefs, etc. Changing your mindset can help the flow of abundance start moving positively in your life.

One of the things I've noticed about my richer friends who are millionaires is they don't worry about money, because they have it. I know it's easy to not worry about money when you already have it, but many of them at one time did not have money. They weren't born into money, but they found work that they loved doing that ultimately brought them a great deal of money. Their mentality was more about diving into their work life passion, then the money just kept rolling in. Successful people don't have negative thoughts about money or making money. Negative self-talk is damaging and blocks abundance from rolling in.

You can scoff, dismiss it, or make an excuse like, "Well, that's easy for them because...."

As soon as you say anything remotely disagreeable with someone else achieving abundance, then a block has formed. Anyone can feel envious at one time or another. Some uncontrollably feel it out of jealousy, where their life is not where they want it to be. Others can feel it if they've been working just as hard if not harder than the more successful one. Feel the envy quickly because it's come on you uncontrollably, but then be aware you're moving into that space, then transform that into something positive. Become motivated by other successes and say something like, "I'm happy for their success. If they can do it, then I can do it too. "

You are your own person with originality and individuality. You have something to offer as everyone has something special to contribute when they're operating from their best selves. Acknowledge the truth that it must seem easier for the more successful person, but train your mind and your thoughts to find something positive to think and feel about that. It doesn't take any effort to whine or criticize. Finding something to praise someone about takes that extra step of work that the ego never wants to do. The ego wants you to feel envy, because it knows this will stall you from your own success. The Darkness despises happy successful people.

Abundance blocks can also be created if you feel as if you don't really need money. Perhaps as a good hearted spiritually minded person, you trained yourself to not want, desire, or long for money. If you convince yourself that you don't care about money, then money won't come to you. Why would something you don't care about be drawn to you?

Maybe you were trained early on to see money as evil and not something that should matter to you. If that's the case, then you'll ensure it won't come into your life. If something doesn't matter to you, then the Universe will make sure you don't get it, because it doesn't matter to you. This mindset may be something you're aware of or it could be buried in your subconscious that you don't even realize it.

"I never have any money" or "I don't care about money." Both sentences are different, but have the same end result. It's pushing money further away from you, whether you're complaining about not having money or that you don't care about it.

Carve out some alone time to connect with God through prayer and meditation. Let your mind wander to all of the circumstances you can think of throughout your life that may have caused an abundance block. Look at the types of relationships you've had with people from family members, to friends, to lovers. Examine your past work life as well as your current work life. Are you stuck at a job you don't like? When did you decide you were stuck in this job? What would it take for you to get what you want in your work life? What would it take for you to get paid more than you make now?

If you work a day job that is not your passion, but you have a career you'd like to have, then what action steps have you taken or can you take to make that dream a reality. Many of the people I spoke to that transitioned from day job to a career informed me they were working on their career during down time when they weren't at this day job. Eventually one day the cards aligned where the career work started to show a financial increase momentum. The finances grew consistently enough to the point that it enabled them to take that leap of faith to quit their day job.

Allow your mind to wander to each and every place in your life an abundance block could've been caused. You can write it down if you choose or mentally sift through each block. As you scrutinize each block, visualize God's white holy light blasting it away like a gigantic waterfall burning it into a dissolve.

For example, when going back to the earlier exercise on viewing your parent's views on money, make note if you are duplicating your own mother or maternal guardian's view on money. If so when did you start duplicating your mother's views on money? Notice if you feel any strain and where that strain is.

Now clear and transmute any strain, tension, other negative feelings away. Do this by visualizing God's white holy light targeting that area and clearing and blasting that toxic energy away in all directions of time.

You can mentally visualize this happening and/or say, *"Please clear any abundance blocks in this area of my life in all directions of time. And so it is."*

Allow this light to dissolve the abundance block now and today. You might notice the changes happening within and around you. Maybe it'll feel like a heaviness or a body shudder. You may feel faintish like the energy was drained from you. You may tear up or have another kind of visceral reaction. A heaviness may occur in one of your chakra areas. There might be something subtle that takes place within you where you know for sure this has taken effect.

Old beliefs about money could be stuck in your current reality and you want to get that out of you. Everywhere you have this feeling of a lack of abundance belief say the following with intention. *"Fill this abundance block with positive light. Clear and transmute this block into positive blessings in all directions of time now."*

Imagine how much money you'd like to see yourself earn through your work and give it to the Universe to take over from there.

Think back to how old you were when you first had stress and negative feelings associated with money. Allow those thoughts to be cleared with this white light and transmute it to heaven now.

It is okay to believe you are worthy of attracting in positive abundance. You do not need to suffer needlessly because of what other people have told you over the course of your life. This about you, your life, and what you set out to do. It is not about anyone else's negative views of success. Know you are worthy of abundance.

I've always had to put effort into whatever it is I wanted, otherwise nothing would happen. I knew early on as a teenager that I couldn't just sit around and hope I'd get that life changing phone call, letter, or doorbell ring. I learned rather quickly that if you want something, you have to go after it. I coupled that with prayer, faith, asking for help, putting in action, then it would transpire. I had optimism over what I wanted and visualized what I wanted. I asked for heavenly help, then paid attention to any signs or clues they were giving me to help make it happen.

Ironically, I've heard from others over the years how my work ethic has inspired them. It's not something I've thought about much. I just find things I want to do, then I dive into it at full force. It is only years later when others point out, "I didn't realize you worked on all these films and wrote all of these books. You've really done so much!"

When it's pointed out, I take a step back and then look back on the trajectory, then it feels overwhelming. Usually I work on something, wrap that up, then find something else to work on, wrap that up, and so on. Years later it's brought to my attention that I've produced a ton of work. When my focus is directed behind me, then I see that it seems like a great deal was accomplished. My focus is typically forward than backwards, so it doesn't feel overwhelming to me to see the decades of hard productive work I've put into my life.

I've been out with numerous people over the years from business to personal, and there is always a certain point when it moves from friendly banter to them getting serious to saying something like, "I have to say I've always admired your go-getting attitude and personality with things. I've talked to this about others and the way you work. I've forever found that inspiring."

I still get surprised hearing that because it's not expected or something I think about. Usually it's about the content of the work and not my actual work ethic. When it's about my passionate drive and work ethic nature, I grow surprised because I never considered that my own hard working nature would inspire someone else. I just dive into what I want to do wholeheartedly and don't think anything of it. In that sense, it's leading by example. It's not talking about it, but just doing it. That's automatically inspiring others by being who you are.

You have the power to turn your dreams into a reality. Your desire starts within you like a seed that's been planted into the Earth to eventually sprout some crops, which metaphorically in this case is the abundance. The seed is also symbolically connected to an idea that's been born within you. This idea is something you crave or desire. You can desire and want something or someone with all your influence, but that doesn't necessarily mean it's going to happen. The idea and desire is still an exceptional place to start in the abundant manifestation process.

It's like the Ace of Wands card in the Tarot that can indicate the start of a brilliant idea, but it's the Two of Wands card that is taking the action on that idea to make it happen. Buildings were not erected out of nowhere, movies don't just appear on screen, music isn't created with the snap of a finger, books don't automatically land on a shelf, and people don't suddenly wake up one morning to find that they're in a relationship with someone. It all starts with an idea and a desire in one person's mind. This is the beginning in the same way God had an idea to create the Universe and what that would entail.

The idea is the beginning stages equivalent to a seed or an egg. Over time it gradually builds becoming something more, as you water and breathe it to life through faith coupled with action steps. When a seed is planted into soil, it grows into a plant as you tend to it regularly. The manifestation process works in the same way.

This dream idea can be temporarily dormant within your mind and soul as you move about your Earthly life. It is waiting to be ignited by you so that you can unleash it and take it to places you never thought possible. Igniting it means allowing this idea to build within you. You are thinking about it regularly, you are visualizing how you see it taking place, and how it is forming. This is before it explodes out of you to the point it can no longer be contained. This idea is similar to a fire starting.

Fire is exciting, enthusiastic, passionate, and action oriented. And as mentioned with the Ace and Two of Wands in the Tarot, the Wands are connected to Fire energy. Fire energy is passion, creativity, and action. Use the Wands suit as a metaphor to bringing your dreams into a reality with all of the blessings and pitfalls that could potentially come out of that.

What you desire is created with your own thoughts. You control what it is you'd like to happen. If you resort to residing in a negative state, and the only things that continue to happen for you seems to be on the negative challenging side, then look deeper into your current processes. Make adjustments with your attitude where needed.

You're in a negative state thinking negative thoughts and feeling negative feelings, then this generates more negative circumstances to happen for you. Whereas someone who is typically a positive person with mostly positive thoughts and feelings finds that things go a bit more swimmingly and smoother than the negative person. This is because you have the power to control what you'd like to happen in your world by the essence of your thoughts and feelings. If you don't like being poor, then convince your mind that you are rich. Think like a rich person regardless if this is your current reality. When you think as if you are poor, then you will remain poor.

This is not just about money, but in spiritual essence as well too. This is the basis of a dream before it comes true. It starts as a seed within you, developing into an egg where it grows and expands as you feed and nourish it to life. This is the incubation stage, then once this egg has developed enough, you begin to take action steps towards making it a reality. The planning stage is like a human pregnancy where it can remain inactive as you develop it for some time, until it's ready to be born. This is when you take action on it to bring what you desire to fruition.

You tend to this dream as if it were your child. Perhaps you keep this dream to yourself, protected and for you only. If you share it, then share it only with those who are optimistic people you trust. Avoid sharing it with someone you know will react negatively. You wouldn't hand your child to a toxic person and you shouldn't do that with your dreams. Think of your dreams as if it's your child.

CHAPTER SIXTEEN

Have Confidence and Ask For Divine Support

*T*here are some that prefer you be meek about your accomplishments. They see boasting about what you've done makes you come off as if you have a big ego. Typically, those that complain or attack others on those matters haven't accomplished much, so it feels like those that have accomplished many things are rubbing it in. You might be thought of as too confident, arrogant, and maybe even a narcissus. Talking about what you've accomplished and the hard work you've put in to making something happen is not arrogant. It's admirable as it shows you have goals, passion, and drive. It indicates that you're a hard worker, you're strong, and you get things done.

Warrior-like go-getters are attracted to other go-getters. Those looking to be inspired are attracted to those go-getters as it inspires them. When you persevere and accomplish your dreams and you succeed, then this is marvelous in the eyes of those who enjoy feeling inspired and motivated. It gives others hope that they can do it too. They know if they set their mind to it and work hard, then they will reach their destination.

When talking about your accomplishments with anyone whether it's in a job interview or with a friend, don't worry about coming off too aggressive. Shout what you've accomplished from the rooftops and don't be fearful about it. Own what you created and fought to make happen.

One of the biggest abundance blocks is a trait that continues to destroy humanity on so many levels, and that is fear. When you have fear of anything in life, then that fear also creates an abundance block. This can be fear of the end of the world being near, or fear over anything associated with the media or politics.

Most of the things you want to run from are the tools you're intended to use to help improve and transform your soul. There is a reason you endure difficult circumstances, whether it's a job you currently don't care for, or a relationship connection that didn't end well. You were gaining wisdom, knowledge, and skills while in those circumstances to take with you to the next venture. Every experience I had, additional tools and traits were gained that would be needed for my next mission, and so on. All experiences you have are not just life changing growth qualities gained, but they happen so that you can apply it to future endeavors.

Abundance is not automatically granted to those that seek and ask for it. There are numerous factors that have to come into play. Sometimes life lessons and experience needs to happen before the rewards come in. Sitting around wishing and hoping for a miracle will generally not bring in the miracle. Tough times are part of the soul's growth process before the floodgates of abundance are cracked open.

Putting in action steps towards your goals can increase your odds of bringing in abundance. This is due to a combination of factors from action movement to the positive excited feelings you have building up inside of you about the endeavor. The universe detects this optimistic energy you radiate outwardly. As you partake in endeavors that have a positive meaning for you, playing an active role in the process will help over doing nothing. It's like the old saying that if you want to increase your chances to winning the lottery, then you have to buy a ticket. It doesn't mean you'll win the lottery, but you have more of a shot than if you didn't buy a ticket. This metaphor is similarly aligned with your dreams.

Going through the list to assist you in attracting in positive abundance, another important step to include is you want to ask for help. If you don't ask for help, then how can the doorway to bring in help be forthcoming? Asking for help includes inviting in God and your Spirit team in your life to work with you daily. Working with you doesn't necessarily mean to grant your wishes like a genie in a bottle, but it is to guide you towards what you need to personally do to help move things along towards positive blessings. This includes the life lessons that will move you towards that doorway of light.

You can verbally ask for God and your Spirit team's help out loud, mentally in prayer, or you can write it out. It doesn't matter how you ask for heavenly help, but that you do. This is due to God's universal free will law that says no higher spirit being in Heaven can assist any soul unless they've been given permission to do so. This doesn't automatically mean that what you are asking for help with will happen or that it will happen right away.

Be as clear as possible with your request, because your Spirit team follows what you ask for. If you are not specific, then you might be surprised by what comes in or doesn't come in. If the request sounds wishy-washy or unclear, then something else may come in that you don't want, or nothing at all will come in. You may even wonder why something came in that you didn't want, but then you recall what you asked for and realize that you indirectly requested it without realizing it.

Think about what you'd like to have or what you'd like to accomplish. Visualize it happening in your mind, then put in daily practice of keeping it there. Let it overflow your entire body, mind, and soul with the essence of that desire. Make a pact to do this daily. You can do this at the start of the day upon waking, at night upon falling asleep, or both. It won't hurt to do it more than once a day.

I was training with weights in a workout with a fitness friend. As I'm lifting I asked, "Should I do another rep?"

He said, "It can't hurt."

This is similar to making your dreams come true. It cannot hurt to give more than you typically give.

Don't worry about not asking for the right thing because requests are not automatically granted like Santa Claus with a sleigh full of gifts. If something is not aligned with your higher self, or if it's something bathed in greed, then it is unlikely to transpire. If it does, then it isn't long before something upsets that balance. This has been witnessed in cases where the greedy that achieve through deceitful means meet their demise at some point in their life.

A man struggled not knowing how to make certain aspects of his life better. I asked him, "Have you tried praying for help?"

He said, "You can pray for something like that?"

I said, "You can pray about anything you like. There are no limits."

He said, "What if it isn't God's will?"

I said, "Then He won't give it to you."

Ask for help and have crystal clear intentions about what you desire. If you feel unsure of what you want, then this can create unsatisfactory results. If you fear asking for the wrong thing, then it is this fear that can manifest as an abundance block.

Other abundance blocks can be fear that you don't deserve help or fears of being selfish, etc. Be sure of what you want and don't hold back for fear of asking for the wrong thing. Don't worry about whether or not your request is a selfish request or not. Your request may be selfish, but your team might not think so. If the request is considered selfish or not aligned with your souls purpose, the wish won't be granted anyway.

Attracting in abundance and the laws of attraction basically say that if you work hard enough with persistence, passion, and optimism, then you can achieve and reach your goals. If you don't try, then you won't have a shot. If you battle with feeling depressed, worthless, or have low self-esteem, then the first steps will be to work on improving your well-being state. If your well-being state is perpetually in a negative state, then first focus on ways to improve that. This is not about someone who has the occasional drop down into negativity, but rather about those who battle uphill in life in that negative state every single day.

Working on improving matters requires your dedication and persistence one day at a time. You implement new strategies and techniques to apply to your life that help dissolve those negative feelings and thoughts you carry around. This is also why taking care of yourself on all levels possible is beneficial. It helps to keep you working on optimum levels, while cracking open the psychic communication line with God. All of this is included as part of the process towards slamming that abundance door wide open.

CHAPTER SEVENTEEN

Giving and Receiving in the Right Spirit

*B*alance giving and receiving energy gestures throughout the course of your day-to-day movements. Giving is not necessarily giving money away, although giving something to your favorite charities definitely counts. Giving is also the giving of a small positive act to another person that has the potential to brighten their day, such as a smile or a compassionate complimentary word or more.

Sometimes it's the little acts of kindness that might go unnoticed, but which are actually creating a wave of love. One person makes one small kind move to help someone. That person carries that act of compassion to another, and so on until it wraps back around reaching the original person again in the end.

What you put out eventually comes back to you. This is seen on the planet with the dark energy, but rarely shown are these small moments of love from others in the seemingly smallest of ways. I notice those little small acts of kindness from others that come through out of that one amazing person out of hundreds.

Once I had dropped a huge wad of cash not realizing it. This guy jogged after me and said, "Excuse me."

I turned around and he had a smile, "You dropped this, here you go."

I said stunned, "What? Thank you. Wait a minute, who does what you just did?"

I handed him some of it as a reward.

He put his hand up refusing it and said, "Just pay it forward."

I smiled, "I will."

Another incident, I was standing at a urinal and this guy tapped me and said, "I think this is yours."

It was my driver's license. These things might be small, but you'd be surprised how rare those small acts of kind gestures are. There are people with ill intentions that might steal it, throw it away, or not bother to say anything.

In 2014, I ended up on crutches for six weeks after tearing the tendon on my foot during a bootleg camp work out accident where I landed on a jump wrong. Everything is fine today as if it never happened, but back then I was balancing on the crutches and putting groceries into my car with another hand. This well-to-do rich woman in her thirties with one of those massive SUV's was loading up her car before she caught my juggling act. Like a fireman answering a bell she gasped and quickly jogged over to me to help. Again you'd be surprised that those little things are rare, so when they happen you do feel the magic of humanity's compassion that is there deep down.

Use God's mantra of remembering to spread more love, more kindness, more compassion, even in those tiny gestures like a smile to a stranger. They add up and do mean something in the eyes of the Universe. You don't do those things for fanfare or attention, but because you have a strong willed compassionate sensitive part of you that cares wanting to be of service.

Those are the little gestures that are actually large blessings you're giving to other people. It doesn't take much to brighten someone's day just from a simple move. Because there isn't enough of it as it is, that when it does happen, whoever is on the receiving end notices it.

I've had people tell me that only one person smiled at them throughout the day, and it was that one person that stood out enough that it uplifted their energy after that. They could feel it shift from a stranger's random genuine smile. Sometimes those reminders are God working through other people to reach out and make that positive move towards someone that could use it at that moment.

Stay strong in faith and know that there is a plan. Pray daily. Ask for help daily. Even if the answer isn't forthcoming right away. It will eventually come. This isn't some blanket statement or enlightenment on a teabag. I speak also through experience.

My first job was when I was seventeen at a popular top record store chain back when those existed. Years in, I was worried I was going to be there forever and would ultimately die there. Obviously that wasn't the case, but I still remember that feeling would plague me while there once in awhile, not everyday. It wasn't that I hated the job. I actually did like it at the time, but it wasn't my life purpose. I had bigger dreams. That's just one example out of many throughout my life. I remember feeling that stagnancy at some point fearing I'd be stuck. I prayed daily and have since I was a child. It's not just to help me with this or that. It's also to express gratitude for what I have at that time in my life that's working.

I've tested God repeatedly since I was a child. I noticed when I didn't pray, then nothing would happen. When I did pray, things got easier, and doors eventually opened. It also wasn't right away each time. There were days that went by where I prayed and nothing would come to light. Months would pass and still nothing. Months turned into years and suddenly out of nowhere the answer that came in was lit up like a Christmas tree and I was placed in an even better set up. There were varying time limits as to when a prayer was answered. For some instances it was immediate, while others took much longer.

If you're in a situation that you don't care for,

there is a reason for it. Sometimes you're in a situation longer than you intended, but you're acquiring skills and traits that God needs you to collect, because it will be useful and beneficial for what's to come next. If you were thrown in what's to come too soon, then it would fail, so He knows when it'll be time. You'll look back and then realize, "Ohhhh now I know why I was there."

Both the good and the bad, everything I've gone through and endured ultimately had a benefit I gained that I was to apply to the next chapter of my life.

You work your day job to survive, but meanwhile you work on your life purpose and passion on the side. When you devote 30-60 minutes a day towards your purpose, then eventually that will grow over time. One day you are making enough income with that enabling you to survive doing it full time. If it's your life purpose work, then it doesn't feel like work. This is because it's your passion and it's enjoyable to dive into.

One of technologies benefits is you can watch instructional videos, seminars, read books, or listen to motivational podcasts right on your computer or phone. You can do it kicking back on the couch after a long day at work. If you're too tired after work to put any effort into your life purpose, then you can do those little action steps where you're gaining knowledge kicking back and watching, reading, or listening to motivational pieces.

Another positive beneficial reason for taking care of yourself on all levels is that it gives you more energy in the day to dive into your purpose, even after working at another job. There are people that work more than one job. Look at your life purpose as a second job if you already have a primary job.

You are sometimes thrown into situations with people that have no connection beyond anything but the superficial. It feels as if you're being tested, but there is a deeper reason for it. You have a light that is working through others even if you don't see that as it's happening or while you're in that situation with them.

I've always been super guarded and cautious over who I allow near me. I can come off aloof and cold when I truthfully have no interest in inviting in those who choose to live in harshness or meanness. I can't even force pretend that I care. I have to keep my own light protected from that darkness.

It's okay to ask for heavenly help in guiding you to an improved situation with loving people you feel more comfortable getting along with, because you deserve it. You deserve to have your prayers answered. Notice any signs or synchronicities of God's help that can sometimes come in a form you weren't expecting as well. It will keep showing up until you notice it and take action on it.

I work for God or as I jokingly say, *God, Incorporated.* Ultimately the abundance is filtered down from Him and into my life in many ways. When I need supplies, I put in a request with Him. Sometimes He grants it and other times He doesn't, but I'm made aware as to if it's just a temporary delay and to be patient, or if it's because He sees that this particular supply I'm asking for will not benefit me positively in the end. My own vision may be limited to the results of what would happen if I received that particular request. Sometimes it's my own ego that desires something, not realizing I could be harmed in the end. Other times there is a temporary delay or He plans to bring in something better that is taking a bit longer to fulfill. This also applies to you as well as anyone interested in how God works.

The enemy will always try to get in there and undo all of the work you've been doing on yourself. You cannot allow that to happen. The enemy is the darkness, the devil, the ego, or the lower self. It doesn't like progress, so it does what it can to stop you by getting into your mind and making you doubt or experience fear. You don't have to endure life alone, since that's where God comes in free of charge whenever you ask.

There is an old song by Sade called, *"King of Sorrow"*, where the lyrics she sang were, "I've already paid for my future sins."

The story in the song describes someone who was working hard and not getting anywhere, but secretly longing for some kind of positive breakthrough release.

Continue to keep the faith and know that things will change one day. Sending you Divine help as you read this now and wishing you the awesome best in life, because you deserve it.

Abundance Exercise

*H*ere is an abundance visualization exercise that you may choose to do or not do daily or whenever you feel like it. You may also choose to expand on it and create your own exercise that works for you over time.

Find a comfortable undisturbed space to lie down on the floor, or in a nature setting, such as a patch of grass in a park or your backyard. If you're in a room, then look up at the ceiling. If you're outside then look up at the sky, pending the sun is not in your eye line.

Imagine the sky or your ceiling opening up letting bright Heavenly Divine light in. It breaks through blasting away all negativity and debris in your midst. Now visualize the sky or ceiling cracking open even more. Visualize infinite money bills falling out of it from God and on top of you while you lay there. You can create an ambiance of candles and listen to some good music as you lay there with a smile visualizing all these riches falling on you from above. These riches also equate to feelings of a strong powerful positive well-being, good friends, great health, lovely home, and a beautiful radiant love partner that you match with the same veracity. You can substitute the money for other desires.

Think about the roadblocks that constantly get in your way of attracting in abundance. It can be your own thoughts and feelings or another person.

As you think about each roadblock that stops the flow of positive abundance, begin putting into practice a visualization exercise. This is one where you close your eyes and imagine those blocks being blasted away with white light. This allows the block to disintegrate and fall away from you to reveal what you've long desired. Imagine each of these roadblocks dissolving away out of your aura.

Remove all mental obstacles of lack and begin to visualize what you want. For example, if you want a house, then visualize this house and the surrounding area of what you would like it to be. What kind of house is it? What does it look like in your imagination?

Visualize yourself walking through the front door of this house and moving through it. Who is in this house with you? Is it a love interest? A man or a woman? What are they like? Are there other people there or is it just you? Imagine this desire as if it's happening and has come true now. Surround yourself and your thoughts with this image in your mind. What you visualize and envision you eventually receive. Through the power of your thoughts and feeling energy, you are bending towards that dream coming true. Do this regularly until the dream has become a reality no matter how long it takes.

The human ego mind sees things as fearful based riddled with negative emotions such as anxiety or depression. The higher self soul sees the potential and capabilities of achieving abundance. Allow abundance to come crashing into your life with welcome open arms.

Tell yourself daily that you are worthy of receiving abundance. You are qualified, worthy, and deserving of good. You are filled up with a never ending overflowing cornucopia of abundance. The floodgates have opened and the door to abundance has slammed open. Light is soaring in with abundant energy all throughout it. This light surrounds you like a great big hug. Abundance is all that it entails from a wonderful relationship, magnificent health, good friendships, etc. It can be feeling abundant spiritually and emotionally.

Move into the alignment that you believe you have everything you could possible want in your life. See it as if it's live and in motion now, even if it hasn't transpired yet. Allow your mind to see that it is. Allow your feelings to sense the great feelings associated with how you would feel to have that life. See and feel it as if it is here with you in your mind now. What will your state of being feel like?

Find that optimistic uplifting space knowing you have all that you could ever want and more. Get your energy into this positive alignment with God now. It surrounds you in a magnetic powerful way that you can feel it as you move about through life. You feel God's magnificent presence working with you to keep this momentum going. You are a powerful magical manifester with the ability to create all that you desire by the actions and energy of your thoughts and feelings. This is your winning card for abundance success. You have these skills within you. Start taking action steps towards attracting what you desire today.

Available in Paperback and E-Book
is the B-Side to the Attracting in Abundance book

ABUNDANCE ENLIGHTENMENT
An Easy Motivational Guide to
the Laws of Attracting in Abundance
and Transforming Your Soul

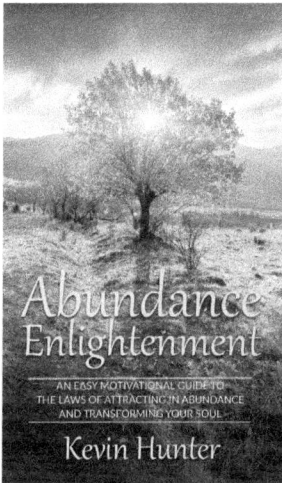

Ultimate authentic success surrounds your soul's growth and evolving process. It's when you realize that none of the physical ego driven desires matter in the end. You can work hard to make sure you stay afloat, you're able to pay your bills, and support yourself and family, but you're not chasing popularity for external validation. Any amount of goodness displayed from your heart is the true measure of real accomplishment.

An overflowing feeling of optimism and love coupled with faith and action is what increases the chances of attracting good things and positive experiences to you. Abundance is more than monetary and financial increase. It can also be about reaching an optimistic well-being state of joy, peace, and love. This positive emotional mindful state simultaneously attracts in blessings.

Abundance Enlightenment is the follow up book to *Attracting in Abundance*. It contains both practical guidance and spirit wisdom that can be applied to everyday life. Some of the key topics surround the laws of attraction as well as healthier money management and improving your soul to help make you a fine tuned in abundance attractor.

ALSO BY KEVIN HUNTER

The Essential Kevin Hunter Collection
Available in Paperback and E-book

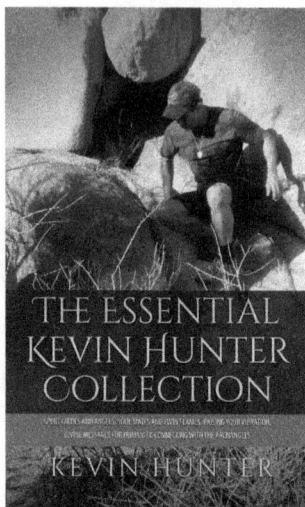

THE ESSENTIAL
KEVIN HUNTER
COLLECTION

Featuring the following books:
Warrior of Light, Empowering Spirit Wisdom, Darkness of Ego,
Spirit Guides and Angels, Soul Mates and Twin Flames, Raising
Your Vibration, Divine Messages for Humanity, and Connecting
with the Archangels.

WARRIOR OF LIGHT
Messages from my Guides and Angels

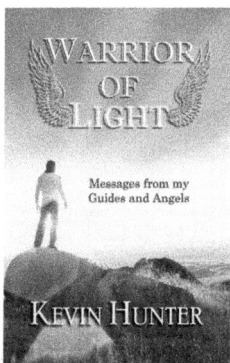

There are legions of angels, spirit guides, and departed loved ones in heaven that watch and guide you on your journey here on Earth. They are around to make your life easier and less stressful. Learn how you can recognize the guidance of your own Spirit team of guides and angels around you. Author, Kevin Hunter, relays heavenly guided messages about getting humanity, the world, and yourself into shape. He delivers the guidance passed onto him by his own Spirit team on how to fine tune your body, soul and raise your vibration. Doing this can help you gain hope and faith in your own life in order to start attracting in more abundance.

EMPOWERING SPIRIT WISDOM
A Warrior of Light's Guide on Love, Career and the Spirit World

Kevin Hunter relays heavenly, guided messages for everyday life concerns with his book, *Empowering Spirit Wisdom*. Some of the topics covered are your soul, spirit and the power of the light, laws of attraction, finding meaningful work, transforming your professional and personal life, navigating through the various stages of dating and love relationships, as well as other practical affirmations and messages from the Archangels. Kevin Hunter passes on the sensible wisdom given to him by his own Spirit team in this inspirational book.

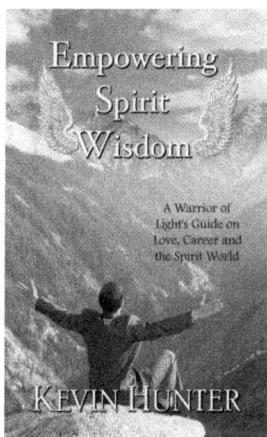

DARKNESS OF EGO

In *Darkness of Ego*, author Kevin Hunter infuses some of the guidance, messages, and wisdom he's received from his Spirit team surrounding all things ego related. The ego is one of the most damaging culprits in human life. Therefore, it is essential to understand the nature of the beast in order to navigate gracefully out of it when it spins out of control. Some of the topics covered in *Darkness of Ego* are humanity's destruction, mass hysteria, karmic debt, and the power of the mind, heaven's gate, the ego's war on love and relationships, and much more.

REACHING FOR THE WARRIOR WITHIN

Reaching for the Warrior Within is the author's personal story recounting a volatile childhood. This led him to a path of addictions, anxiety and overindulgence in alcohol, drugs, cigarettes and destructive relationships. As a survival mechanism, he split into many different "selves". He credits turning his life around, not by therapy, but by simultaneously paying attention to the messages he has been receiving from his Spirit team in Heaven since birth.

REALM OF THE WISE ONE

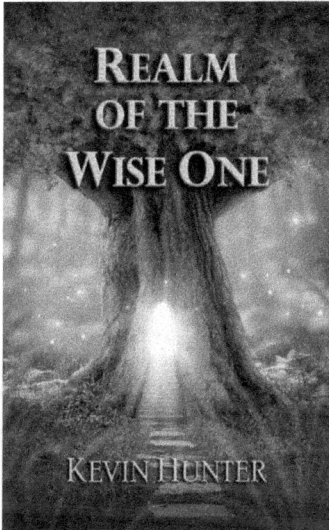

In the Spirit Worlds and the dimensions that exist, reside numerous kingdoms that house a plethora of Spirits that inhabit various forms. One of these tribes is called the Wise Ones, a darker breed in the spirit realm who often chooses to incarnate into a human body one lifetime after another for important purposes.

The *Realm of the Wise One* takes you on a magical journey to the spirit world where the Wise Ones dwell. This is followed with in-depth and detailed information on how to recognize a human soul who has incarnated from the Wise One Realm. Author, Kevin Hunter, is a Wise One who uses the knowledge passed onto him by his Spirit team of Guides and Angels to relay the wisdom surrounding all things Wise One. He discusses the traits, purposes, gifts, roles, and personalities among other things that make up someone who is a Wise One. Wise Ones have come in the guises of teachers, shaman, leaders, hunters, mediums, entertainers and others. *Realm of the Wise One* is an informational guide devoted to the tribe of the Wise Ones, both in human form and on the other side.

TRANSCENDING UTOPIA

Available in Paperback and E-book

Transcending Utopia is packed with practical and spirit knowledge that focuses on enhancing your life through empowering divinely guided spiritual related teachings, inspiration, wisdom, guidance, and messages. The way to accelerate existence on Earth towards Utopia is if every person on the planet resided in their soul's true nature, which is in a state of all love, joy, and peace. The ultimate Nirvana is surpassing that perfection through methods that a limited consciousness could ever dream possible. This is the exceptional glory your soul was born into before the dense turbulence of Earthly life enveloped and suffocated you.

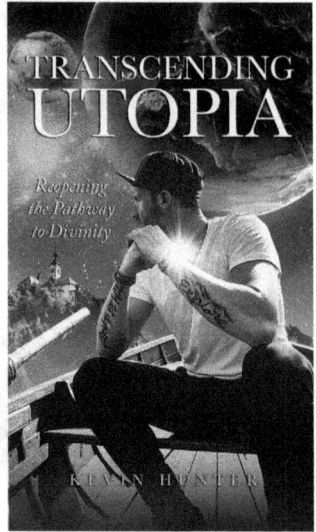

Transcending Utopia is to go beyond your limits and travel outside of the generic mundane materialistic achievement that human beings taught one another to thrive for. A utopian society is where everything is perfectly blissful on all levels according to the sanctified values you were born with. The sensations connected to how flawless everything feels in that moment reveals the authentic perfection you were made from. Utopia is the ideal paradise as imagined in one's dreams that seems to be inaccessible by human standards. It is a state of mind that is possible to reach by adopting broader ways of looking at circumstances while being disciplined about how you conduct your life. You search for a sign of this utopia through external means, only to be consistently left with disappointment. This is because utopia begins and ends inside the spark that burns within your spirit like a pilot light waiting to be ignited.

Living for the Weekend

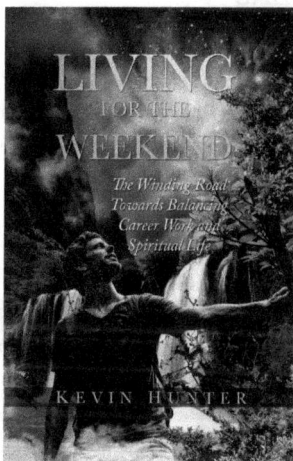

The Winding Road Towards Balancing Career Work and Spiritual Life

Available in Paperback and E-book

Working hard to ensure your bills are paid can leave your soul spiritually starved for soul nourishment. When your ultimate goal is to obtain enough money to be comfortable that you become carried away in that current, then there is little to no room for Divine enrichment.

Many work to survive in jobs they hate because it's the way it is. As a result, they experience and endure all sorts of emotional pain whether it is through depression, sadness, anger, or any other kind of negative stressor. Some silently suffer through this emotional strain gradually killing off their life force. If you don't have a healthy social life and positive fun filled activities and hobbies to balance that burden outside of that, then that can add additional tension. What's it all for if you can't live the life you've always wanted to live? Instead, you spend your days growing forever miserable and broken.

Living for the Weekend examines the pitfalls, struggles, as well as the benefits available in the current modern day working world. This is followed up with spiritual and practical tips, guidance, messages, and discussions on ways to incorporate more balance and enlightenment to a cutthroat material driven world.

MONSTERS
AND ANGELS

*An Empath's Guide to Finding Peace in a Technologically Driven
World Ripe with Toxic Monsters and Energy Draining Vampires*

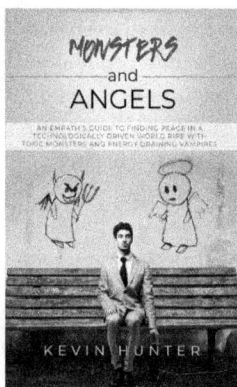

Every person on the planet is capable of being empathic and sensitive, to becoming an energy vampire or toxic monster. No one is exempt from displaying the darker sides of their ego. The easiest and most efficient way to spread any kind of energy is online. Every time you log onto the Internet, there is a larger chance you're going to see something related to the news, media, or gossip areas thrown in front of you, even if you attempt to avoid it as much as possible. You're absorbing everything that your consciousness faces, including the ugly and the wicked, which has its own consequences. This tempestuous energy is tossed into the Universe ultimately creating a flame-throwing battleground inside and around you.

Monsters and Angels discusses how technology, media, and social media have an immense power in distributing both positive and negative influences far and wide. This is about being mindful of what can negatively affect your state of being, and how to counter and avoid that when and wherever possible. This is why it's beneficial to govern yourself, your life, and your surroundings like a strict disciplined executive.

Twin Flame Soul Connections

Recognizing the Split Apart, the Truths and Myths of Twin Flames, Soul Love Connections, Soul Mates, and Karmic Relationships

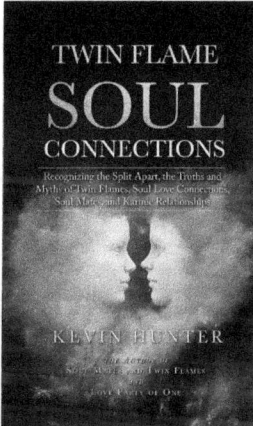

Twin Flames have a shared ongoing sentiment and quest from the moment they're a spark shooting out of God's love that explodes into a blinding white fire that breaks apart causing one to be two, until two become one again, separate and whole, and back around again. Looking into the eyes of your Twin Flame is like looking into the eyes of God, because to know love is to know God.

When one thinks of a Soul Mate or Twin Flame, they might equate it to a passionate romantic relationship where you're making love on a white sandy palm tree lined beach in paradise for the rest of your lives. This beautiful mythological notion has caused great turmoil in others who long for this person that fits the description of a lothario character in a romance novel. It is also an unrealistic and misguided interpretation of the Soul Mate or Twin Flame dynamic.

Twin Flame Soul Connections discusses and lists some of the various myths and truths surrounding the Twin Flames, and how to identify if you've come into contact with your Twin Flame, or if you know someone who has. The ultimate goal is not to find ones Twin Flame, but to awaken ones heart to love, and to work on becoming complete and whole as an individual soul through spiritual self-mastery, life lessons, growth, and raising your consciousness. Your soul's life was born out of love and will die right back into that love.

IGNITE YOUR INNER LIFE FORCE

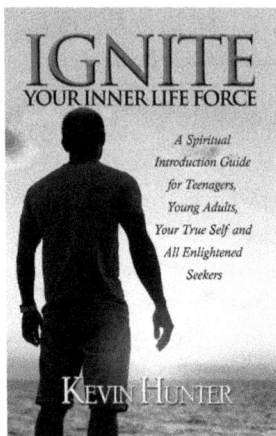

Ignite Your Inner Life Force is an introduction guide for teens, young adults, and anyone seeking answers, messages, and guidance and surrounding spiritual empowerment. This is from understanding what Heaven, the soul, and spiritual beings are to knowing when you are connecting with your Spirit team of Guides and Angels. Some of the topics covered are communicating with Heaven, working with your Spirit team, what your higher self is, your life purpose and soul contract, what the ego is, love and relationships, your vibration energy, shifting your consciousness and thinking for yourself even when you stand alone. This is an in-depth primer manual offering you foundation as you find a higher purpose navigating through your personal journey in today's modern day practical world.

AWAKEN YOUR CREATIVE SPIRIT

Your creative spirit is more than being artistic and getting involved in creativity pursuits, although this is a good part of it. When your creative spirit is activated by a high vibration state of being, then this is the space you create from. You can apply this to your dealings in life, your creative and artistic pursuits, and to having a greater communication line with your Spirit team on the Other Side. *Awaken Your Creative Spirit* is an overview of what it means to have access to Divine assistance and how that plays a part in arousing the muse within you in order to bring your state of mind into a happier space.

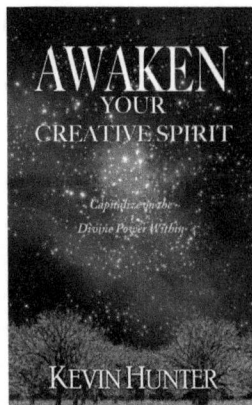

The *Warrior of Light* series of pocket books are available in paperback and E-book called, *Spirit Guides and Angels, Soul Mates and Twin Flames, Divine Messages for Humanity, Raising Your Vibration, Connecting with the Archangels,* and *The Seven Deadly Sins*

TAROT CARD MEANINGS

A Beginner's Guide to the
FOUR PSYCHIC CLAIR SENSES

Learn about the four main psychic clair senses to help you connect with Heaven, the Spirit World, and the Other Side. Take that one step further and use those senses to read the Tarot! *Tarot Card Meanings* is an encyclopedia reference guide that takes the Tarot apprentice reader through each of the 78 Tarot Cards offering the potential general meanings and interpretations that could be applied when conducting a reading, whether it be spiritual, love, general, or work related questions. This is an easy to understand manual for the Tarot novice that is having trouble interpreting cards for themselves, or a Tarot reader who loves the craft and is looking for a refresher or another point of view. The *Four Psychic Clair Senses* focuses on the main channels that Heaven and Spirit communicate with you. *Both books are available in Paperback and E-book wherever books are sold.*

About Kevin Hunter

Kevin Hunter is the metaphysical spiritual author of more than two-dozen spiritually based books that tackle a variety of genres and tend to have a strong male protagonist. The messages and themes he weaves in his work surround Spirit's own communications of love and respect, which he channels and infuses into his writing work.

His spiritually based empowerment books include *Warrior of Light, Empowering Spirit Wisdom, Realm of the Wise One, Reaching for the Warrior Within, Darkness of Ego, Transcending Utopia, Living for the Weekend, Ignite Your Inner Life Force, Awaken Your Creative Spirit,* and *Tarot Card Meanings.* His metaphysical pocket books series include, *Spirit Guides and Angels, Soul Mates and Twin Flames, Raising Your Vibration, Divine Messages for Humanity, Connecting with the Archangels, The Seven Deadly Sins, Four Psychic Clair Senses, Monsters and Angels, Twin Flame Soul Connections, Attracting in Abundance,* and *Abundance Enlightenment.* He is also the author of the dating singles guide *Love Party of One,* the horror/drama, *Paint the Silence,* and the modern day erotic love story, *Jagger's Revolution.*

Kevin started out in the entertainment business in 1996 as the personal development guy to one of Hollywood's most respected talent, Michelle Pfeiffer, for her boutique production company, Via Rosa Productions. She dissolved her company after several years and he made a move into coordinating film productions for the studios on such films as *One Fine Day, A Thousand Acres, The Deep End of the Ocean, Crazy in Alabama, The Perfect Storm, Original Sin, Harry Potter & the Sorcerer's Stone, Dr. Dolittle 2,* and *Carolina.* He considers himself a beach bum born and raised in Southern California. For more information: www.kevin-hunter.com